"What Would Make You Happy, Everett?"

she asked as she held the key poised over the lock of her door. "I really want to know."

He shifted his weight as if he were preparing to take her in his arms. Then she saw something pass over his eyes. A mask? A warning?

A quick, sad smile curved the edges of his mouth. "You would make me happy," he said thickly and turned abruptly on his heel.

He didn't look back as she watched him walk away.

LINDA SHAW

is the mother of three children and enjoys her life in Keene, Texas, which she shares with her husband. When Linda isn't writing romantic novels, she's practicing or teaching the piano, violin, or viola.

Dear Reader:

Silhouette has always tried to give you exactly what you want. When you asked for increased realism, deeper characterization and greater length, we brought you Silhouette Special Editions. When you asked for increased sensuality, we brought you Silhouette Desire. Now you ask for books with the length and depth of Special Editions, the sensuality of Desire, but with something else besides, something that no one else offers. Now we bring you SILHOUETTE INTIMATE MOMENTS, true romance novels, longer than the usual, with all the depth that length requires. More sensuous than the usual, with characters whose maturity matches that sensuality. Books with the ingredient no one else has tapped: excitement.

There is an electricity between two people in love that makes everything they do magic, larger than life—and this is what we bring you in SILHOUETTE INTIMATE MOMENTS. Look for them wherever you buy books.

These books are for the woman who wants more than she has ever had before. These books are for you. As always, we look forward to your comments and suggestions. You can write to me at the address below:

Karen Solem
Editor-in-Chief
Silhouette Books
P.O. Box 769
New York, N.Y. 10019

LINDA SHAW
Way of the Willow

Silhouette Special Edition

Published by Silhouette Books New York

America's Publisher of Contemporary Romance

Other Silhouette Books by Linda Shaw

December's Wine
All She Ever Wanted
After the Rain

 SILHOUETTE BOOKS, a Simon & Schuster Division of
GULF & WESTERN CORPORATION
1230 Avenue of the Americas, New York, N.Y. 10020

ISBN: 0-671-53597-8

First Silhouette Books printing June, 1983

10 9 8 7 6 5 4 3 2 1

All of the characters in this book are fictitious. Any resemblance to actual persons, living or dead, is purely coincidental.

Map by Ray Lundgren

Way of the Willow

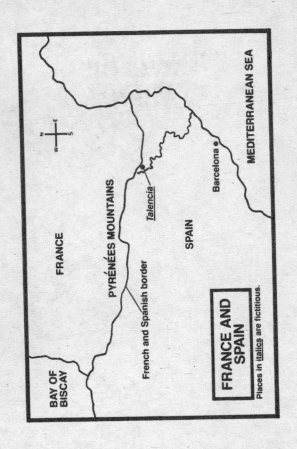

FRANCE AND SPAIN

Places in _italics_ are fictitious.

FRANCE

SPAIN

BAY OF BISCAY

PYRÉNÉES MOUNTAINS

French and Spanish border

Talencia

Barcelona

MEDITERRANEAN SEA

Chapter One

On a morning so tightly structured that the slightest irregularity could send her plans crashing down like a house of cards, Jennifer Howard heard the roar of Bartlett Street's voice. She glanced up from her drafting board to see him sweep a Fifth Avenue overcoat from his spare multimillionaire's shoulders. In a gesture calculated to intimidate his listener, he glared down the length of a narrow hawk-shaped nose.

"This isn't what I want, Miss Chase! What kind of a business are you running? I told your assistant sitting over there, Miss . . . What's-her-name, that I wanted the same kind of wall covering the TurtleBank Condominiums are using. And she gives me this. It won't do, Miss Chase. It simply *will not do.*"

The owner of Chase Interiors wilted at the sight of the obnoxious, middle-aged architect venting his complaints. She was a moderately small woman, at least ten years his junior. Pamela tended to mistrust all men in general, especially ones whose wealth was measured in eight digits and whose voices reached a booming decibel level.

"There's no need to be upset, Mr. Street," she said uneagerly. "Our job is to please you."

"Then do it!"

Pamela Chase glanced across the office to the opposite desk, where her assistant sat, curved over a drafting board, to all appearances deep in concentration, her pencil moving with broad, confident strokes. "Jenny?"

Jenny lifted a curly head at the sound of her name. She peered over the top of efficient wire-frame glasses and arranged her lips in a courteous smile. Bartlett Street was responsible for some of the finest town house developments in Greater Atlanta. He was also Chase Interior's newest client. And, she guessed, he was about to throw one of his famous temper tantrums. It couldn't come at a worse time.

Sighing, preserving her smile, Jenny removed her glasses and slipped off her stool. In two hours she had one of the most important appointments of her life. And Pamela turned into a mental case every time Bartlett Street walked into the office. Well, someone had to pacify him or the account would probably be lost. Wasn't that what assistants were created to be—the proverbial whipping boys, patsies, scapegoats, and chumps in general?

Jenny smoothed the skirt of her modest tweed suit. She walked across the room as if the architect could not buy and sell her kind a dozen times a day.

"Why, Mr. Street," she purred, "how industrious you are." She stole a glance at her wristwatch. "At nine thirty in the morning."

"Time is money," snapped Street.

Pamela offered the pacing man a chair. When he withered her with a scowl, she stood meekly scraping her charm along its chain.

"Well, I don't know what wall covering Jennifer showed you," she said squeakily, continuing to look at Jenny, "but if she's given you advice, I'm sure it's good, Mr. Street. She's almost never wrong about those things." Then, to Jenny, in a tone even less confident, she implored, "Do you know what he's talking about?"

If she missed her commuter train into Atlanta, Jenny thought grimly over the sound of Pamela's scraping and Bartlett's complaining, she couldn't possibly keep her appointment at the bank. And if she missed her appointment at the bank, there would be no down payment for the house. If Jenny couldn't raise a down payment for the house, she couldn't put the boys in a better school or open the antique shop for her mother. The chain reaction would end in the same stagnant pattern of her twenty-eight-year-old existence—raising two young sons who had lost their father in Southeast Asia and supporting a mother who'd lived with her for the last eight years.

"Of course I know what he's talking about," she said, and extended her hand. "I know every detail of Mr. Street's account."

Bartlett stared down at the petite interior decorator, whose slender proportions barely reached his shoulder. He had forgotten how attractive she was with her arresting brown eyes and cap of curly, russet hair. Taking her proffered hand, he watched the unevenness of her lower teeth when she showed them and the dimples in her cheeks, which flashed with an appeal that fascinated him. His scowl relented its ferocity.

"I distinctly remember telling you, Miss . . ."

"*Mrs.* Howard," Jenny reminded pleasantly.

"Ah, yes. Mrs. Howard—The Mother." He lifted her hand to his lips.

After his chivalrous kiss, which was meant to disarm her to the point of agreeing with him, Jenny tactfully disengaged herself. "Now, about the wall covering . . ."

"Two boys, wasn't it? Let me see now . . . aged seven and eight. Am I right?"

"Jeffrey is ten and Stephen is nine, Mr. Street."

Bartlett's eyebrows, when they shot upward, overpowered every other feature of his face. "Really? I'm usually quite good at details like that."

"You have a great many details to remember, which is why I've double-checked everything we talked about. Now, I was in the TurtleBank condos the other day, Mr. Street, and that wallpaper was—"

Jenny consulted her wristwatch again. Suddenly realizing that the only way to save her appointment with Alan Kendall at the bank was to provide Bartlett Street with visible proof, she captured the tall man's hands as he waved several swatches of wallpaper samples.

"I have an idea," she said with forced enthusiasm. "Let's drive over to TurtleBank. It won't take but a minute. I couldn't live with myself if I squandered your money for the sake of convenience, Mr. Street."

At the mention of his money the millionaire swiftly became more docile. Shrugging elaborately, receiving an eager nod of encouragement from Pamela Chase, Bartlett tossed out another of his gestures that Jenny was sure he practiced before a mirror.

"After you, my lovely. Seeing is believing, as they say."

"Let us hope so."

Bartlett's enthusiasm paled, however, when Jenny grabbed up her coat, stepped out into the raw January wind, and proceeded to lead him and his assistant, Clarence, to a Volkswagen Rabbit parked behind the decorator shop. He stood glaring down at it, his talented hands braced on his sides.

"You expect me to ride in that . . . *creature?*" he croaked.

Jenny was freezing. Her smile was maintained only by sheer desperation. "It's the only creature I have, Mr. Street."

Muttering an unintelligible remark under his breath —an epithet Jenny supposed she was blessed for not hearing—Bartlett strode vigorously to his Cadillac Seville parked on the street. He opened the door, flourished another of his rehearsed gestures, and invited Jenny to slide across the plush velour seat.

"We'll go like civilized people," he said.

Then go, she prayed as Bartlett veered out into bustling traffic some twenty-five miles on the outskirts of Atlanta. *And please hurry.*

A mere three blocks before they reached the TurtleBank condominiums, Bartlett Street slowed the Cadillac to a crawl. He worked his brows as he peered over his assistant's shoulder at a valuable acre of corner property with a moldy three-story house centered in the lot.

Jenny knew, with unerring intuition, exactly what he was thinking. She wanted to say, *You can't have this house; it's my dream.* But she only gazed beneath lowered lids at the unsightly weeds, dead from the past summer, the bright-yellow For Sale sign monopolizing the yard. She watched people braving the cold and rushing up the sidewalk to ring the bell. She wondered if living in the house again was a hopeless illusion. She dreamed of having the old house back the way some women dreamed of having a lover. Part of it dated back to the Civil War—the part that Sherman's fiery escapade through Georgia hadn't succeeded in burning. The destroyed portion had been restored after a fashion, but it never had been the landmark that it could be. She wanted to restore it herself, not only because of its history but—she rarely admitted it to herself— because of her own.

"Now, there's a piece of prime property." Bartlett was leaning forward toward the windshield. "Make a note of that, Clarence. That old place is for sale again. Always did think a quadrangle of exclusive shops would do well on this street. Boutiques, salons, collectors' shops. What d'you think, Mrs. Howard? Would you be interested in taking on a project that large?"

Jenny started, her composure faltering. "Oh, I'm always ready for a project, Mr. Street." He couldn't even *think* of tearing down that house. "Personally, I think we should keep a few of these old places."

Bartlett shot her a queer glance in his rearview mirror.

"For our heritage," she mumbled.

"Where's your sense of progress, my dear? Look at it, it's nothing but an eyesore. Weeds veranda-high. That grotesque willow tree. Such a pity!" He clucked dolefully to himself.

Was it a pity? she wondered. Was it pure sentimentality to want to preserve the huge drooping willow tree that had plagued the electrical company for decades by growing into its wires? Perhaps. But the willow tree was a special tree: her undying friend, a comfort when times were bad. When she was nine her father had built her a tree house in it. From its height she'd gazed out upon the town like a ruling queen on a throne. She'd dreamed of being a movie star like Sally Field. Then there was her sixteenth birthday when Everett Black had wheedled her beneath its dainty green fronds. He'd been the first boy who'd ever kissed her.

"I love you," he had vowed, flushed, laughing down at her, trapped so willingly in his arms. "Say you love me, too, Jenny Stephenson. Swear you'll love me forever."

Looking back upon it, she and Everett had been naive children caught in the throes of a desire that had quickly become very adult, very dangerous. Their laughter dwindled as Everett drew her against the hard angles of a body that, at eighteen, was already that of a virile man. At first she resisted his delicate, wispy kisses; she clamped her mouth tightly shut and refused to close her eyes. And he, thinking she didn't want it, halfheartedly let her go. It was her hesitation that made him bold. When her arms twined timidly about his neck and she raised on the tips of her toes, he fastened his lips to hers with a fierceness that reversed everything. Then it was her eyes that closed and her lips that parted. Dazed, a fragile, brown-haired, brown-eyed wren, she'd allowed Everett to take the soft virgin territory of her mouth.

"Do you love me?" he urged, the vigor of youthful arousal hoarse in his voice.

"I'll always love you," she whispered. "I swear it."

For two years she'd loved him blindly. Every teenage fantasy had revolved around Everett, every waking hour. She had painfully watched him go off to college and waited for his return during the long summer days. Then, there had been the burning secret they shared of hot, consuming nights by the lake. She had responded so eagerly and he had outgrown her so gradually, she had hardly known what was happening.

She'd never told anyone about what she and Everett had done, not even Martin when they married. If Martin had guessed he wasn't the first man, he never said so. She'd been a good, faithful wife. Then he, too, was tragically gone.

"You see, Mr. Street," Jenny pointed out when they were strolling through the open house at TurtleBank, "though this covering is beautiful and would work well in another climate, year-round air-conditioning dries it out." She flicked at a peeling section near a window sash, another at a baseboard.

"Perhaps it's the cement they used."

She shook her head. "I checked that out. This covering needs a more humid atmosphere."

"Well, I have to agree that this particular example doesn't live up to its advertising."

"It would have to be replaced before three years."

Subdued, the millionaire turned to his assistant. "How much would that have cost me, Clarence?"

Clarence whipped out a pocket calculator and punched in a few digits. Studying it for a moment, he handed it to his employer.

Bartlett peered down at it, took a short breath, and puckered his outlandish eyebrows.

"Could I take you out to dinner, my dear?" he asked. "Buy you a Dior gown, perhaps, or a Mercedes, so you won't have to drive around in that ghastly golf cart?"

Laughing, knowing that whatever he paid Clarence was money well spent, Jenny gave his arm a fond pat. "I'm just doing my job."

"Could you use a father for your children?" he teased. He suddenly found her and her expertise delightful.

Jenny ran her fingers through her curls in a self-conscious manner. "Don't joke about things like that, Mr. Street."

"Call me Bart. What's the matter, son trouble?"

"The older was sent home from school yesterday for fighting. That"—she looked back over her shoulder as they walked to his Seville—"is something that needs a man's hand."

"Jeffrey?"

She laughed. "You got it right this time."

Bartlett opened her door. "Well, I gather there's someone already in line for the position of father."

When he started the engine with a swift snarl of power, she saw him questioning her in the mirror, waiting for her answer.

"Just barely," she murmured, and sent a fond glance toward her house as they passed.

"It sounds to me like you need to fall in love and get married, young lady."

Jenny didn't reply. She'd been married. She might even marry again. But she had loved only once, an eternity ago, beneath a faithful old tree that everyone thought had outlived its usefulness. She would never love again.

Jenny had promised Pamela she would return from the bank as quickly as she could. The wind whipped across the streets with a numbing vengeance, tossing debris onto the windshield as she sped the dozen blocks to catch the commuter train to Atlanta. If, just once, the 10:35 would be late, she might be in time to catch it. She began to grow doubtful, however, as two red-and-white-striped guardrails began lowering across Main Street when she was only a block from the train terminal. The great diesel engine rumbled in the distance and mingled its warning blast with that of the wind.

Damn Bartlett Street's wallpaper! And the commuter, too, for being on time! She considered turning onto Ferris Street at the next block and outrunning the train. With luck, she could still buy her ticket in time to board.

Throwing a determined glance over her shoulder, she tortured the gears and slammed her foot hard onto the accelerator. She darted past a van and made a turn from a wrong lane.

"Hey, wadda you think you're doin', lady?" yelled the driver before he angrily blared his horn at her. "Wake up!"

Sorry, mister, she silently apologized, *I'm desperate.* Praying she wouldn't get caught for speeding, she raced down Ferris and sped up Third Street. Just as the guardrail began lowering across Third, the Volkswagen bounced across the tracks, turned, and screeched its brakes on the parking lot of the small outlying terminal.

She'd done it! She switched off the key and grabbed her handbag and a small leather portfolio. Climbing out of the seat, she scrambled from the car. The temperature was two degrees above freezing. Her coat swiped against the side of the car as she locked the door. Flicking at the grime that clung to the material, she hurried toward the door of the depot. Once inside, she nearly collided with a man as he stepped out of one of the glass-fronted telephone booths near the entrance.

"Watch it." He grabbed her arms to steady her.

"Sorry," she murmured without even looking at him. She craned over his shoulder to peer at the ticket window. At least there wouldn't be anyone in front of her.

"Give me a ticket to the city, May!" she demanded breathlessly as she rushed to the ticket window.

Jenny rummaged in her bag for money as her marvelous, overweight, laughing friend from high school days reached into a pigeonhole for a roundtrip fare.

"In a hurry, huh?" giggled May. She slammed a date stamp on the ticket. "It's contagious this morning. Everyone's in a hurry. You're all going to suffer from ulcers before you're forty. You know that, don't you? How're the boys?"

"Jeffrey's giving me gray hair. Stephen wants to build an airplane." She drew a circle in the air. "A real one."

Absorbed in watching the train brake into the station, Jenny flipped through her wallet. She considered how much would be left before she withdrew a ten-dollar bill. May counted out her change and pushed it forward across the slick surface of the counter.

"What'd you think of him? How about that, gliding in here like he owned the place and saying he was in Atlanta on business and was looking up a few old friends. He asked about Bob Crandall. Asked about you too."

Coins jingling as she scooped them up, Jenny smiled at her friend and turned toward the door, all in the same movement. The public address system began droning its chant of departures before May's remark began to register. Jenny's chin came down, and her head tilted. She peered over her shoulder.

"Who asked about me?"

May observed Jennifer Stephenson Howard with indulgent eyes. She swept over the clear-skinned face and its dimples. To her, Jenny was an ideal. Professional-looking clothes had sprouted from her sewing machine for years, as if by magic. She held down a rather decent job. She paid the rent on a nice house for her boys and her mother, and, above all else, she was as slender as a reed. It was inconceivable that someone as clever as Jenny didn't know whom she meant.

"Ev-er-ett," May announced with precision. "Everett Black, honey bun. You ran right into the man."

Jenny had already started for the station door. She turned to May, disbelief quivering in her voice. "That man, the one in the suit . . ." she flicked her fingers in the general vicinity of a man's lapels, "*that* was Everett Black?"

May beamed. "He hasn't changed much, has he?" She swiveled her head back and forth. "Quite a hunk."

Changed? Everett Black? The name toppled in Jenny's mind like a domino, striking one memory after another—wonderful, horrible, heart-stopping memories.

"I d-didn't see him that well," she stammered distractedly.

She started to ask what May had told Everett, but a woman bustled in front of her, dragging an inordinate amount of luggage on a carryall. Lifting her eyebrows at the sight of it, May fluttered a haphazard wave at Jenny and slapped the date on another ticket.

Everett Black? thought Jenny. Oh, God, how was that possible? The past couldn't resurrect itself like that with no warning. If Everett were here, in this place, he wouldn't be the past any longer. He would be the present. Everett Black in her present would give it a dangerous dimension she simply could not bear to face the second time.

The conductor was putting the portable step into place and taking tickets. The diesel engine waited, its great generators purring. The ding, ding, ding of the signal lights could be heard from the street.

Jenny began threading her way through the people moving toward the boarding area, but the shock of what May had told her cruelly turned back the calendar. She saw herself naked in Everett's arms. She saw them clinging desperately. She heard him groan in her ear, "It'll be all right, sweetheart. I promise. Just love me, love me."

She surrendered to a wild instinct she trusted absolutely. She had to get out of there!

Quickly she ducked her head and lifted her hand to her temple in an effort to conceal her face. Someone jostled her shoulder and tipped her off balance. Clutching her portfolio, Jenny found herself pushed into yet another person. Her eyes fell immediately upon the sharp creases of pinstriped trousers, the shine of expensive black leather shoes. She smelled the drugging scent of Lagerfeld. She didn't even have to look up to know who it was.

"Oh!"

Though he looked down at her with puzzled blue eyes, only an embryonic speck of recognition in their clear depths, the burn of embarrassment flooded Jenny's throat and cheeks. *What do I say?* she foundered in her mind. *How nice to see you, Everett. How unexpected. I think I've learned to hate you.*

Since she felt everything, she could say nothing.

In that moment Everett reached out a hand to steady her, but he withdrew it without touching. A vague amusement twitched at the edges of his wide, sensually drawn mouth.

His face wasn't too different after all the years. She saw much in her fleeting glance: the black hair that was as sooty and rebellious as ever, his nose as perfectly defined, the cheekbones as high and cleanly planed. His eyes had changed a lot; their blue was more cynical, more wary. And his mouth, though as pleasantly curved as always, seemed tempered with a hint of disillusionment.

It was his air of success that was most striking, perhaps—the way it sat upon the width of his shoulders: competent, a little tough, ultimately cosmopolitan, far removed from her pace of life. His body revealed a harsh discipline with its flat stomach and slender hips and lean, runner's legs. Jenny imagined that most people thought twice before crossing Everett Black and that very few had the courage to discover the man inside the man. She was sure she didn't want to. She couldn't!

He gave her a casual wink and hesitated, as if grappling with impressions long buried in his memory. "It's all right, dear. I think I'm in love."

He had no idea of the perfect cruelty of his jest, she knew. But she felt like a thief caught in a transgression by a whole roomful of people.

"You said that to me once before." Averting her face before his recognition could dawn, she tried to step around him.

"Pardon?"

"I'm sorry."

Meaning to dart past him to the train where she could find the restroom and collect her wits, she twisted her shoulder and started out another way.

"Wait!"

She brushed at the insistent fingers that closed into the sleeve of her coat. "My train—"

"What you said—"

"I'll miss my train. Please, I'm terribly sorry." She practically raced for the double glass doors where half a dozen passengers were passing through to catch the 10:35.

All morning Everett Black had been preoccupied. From the moment he'd stepped off the plane and rented a car, hundreds of details had plagued him. He hadn't been to Atlanta since his college days. After he met and married Ruth in Boston, he'd never come back. He hadn't felt the need. Then he and Ruth had separated and divorced. Returning home now was inhumane in a way—all those poignant, aching memories that he'd never missed very much until he saw them as they had been, all the futile reminders that the years were going by and he was still locked into his familiar circle of solitude.

He was here to review a list of properties his staff in Boston had compiled for him. The pattern was a practiced one by now: He met with the financiers, the philanthropists, the people with the grants. His staff organized the necessary group of research scientists and generated as much public support as possible. He bought the property himself and got the physical plant going. One had been a complex in Nigeria for researching sickle-cell anemia, the last a genetics laboratory in Spain. One of the scientists had gotten a Nobel prize out of that one. It was an impossible job, riddled with enormous pressures and few personal gratifications once it was finished. But it was infinitely worthwhile, and he somehow managed to badger it into workable order at the last moment. This newest project outside Atlanta would be a cancer laboratory. Just now he'd been making last-minute phone calls to realtors and setting up appointments.

He caught up with her as she was reaching the door. "Just a minute," he said.

When she spun about to face him, Everett was shocked to see his past carved in the grief of her face. He saw his own youthful mistakes traced in the pinched corners of her mouth. He knew exactly who she was. She was lovely, but she wasn't a girl anymore; she had to be in her late twenties.

His lips slackened. "Jen . . . Jenny?"

She looked as if her bones had turned to liquid. "I—I have to catch that train, Everett."

She stepped past him.

His step was longer than hers; he moved around her and blocked her path. "Wait!"

From habit he'd put authority in his tone, an edge that he knew defied resistance. When she stopped, lowering her portfolio, he expected her to say something caustic. She had, after all, been trying to avoid him.

Feeling uncharacteristically awkward, he drew on a convenient winsomeness. "You can't leave without saying 'Why, Everett Black, you're the last person in the whole world I expected to see.'" He wondered if she had any idea how good she looked to him.

She hesitated for a moment and, to his surprise, relented. Her dimples twinkled, and she smiled. Shrugging, she said, "'Time is like a fashionable host . . .'"

Reminiscing, he touched his forehead. "Ahh . . . 'That slightly shakes his parting guest by the hand.'"

"You remembered."

"English Lit., Miss Pruitt."

"She's still teaching."

"Her gold watch pinned on the front of her dress?"

"Probably."

They laughed uneasily, breathlessly, then gradually grew solemn again.

Everett moistened his lips. "I remember a lot of things, Jennifer Stephenson. It's been a while, hasn't it?"

"It's Jennifer Howard now, Everett."

He drew a thumbnail across his jaw, then smiled again, thinly. "Of course."

What had he thought? she wondered. That she would not lead her own life just as he had lived his?

"Well, Jenny Howard, life's been very kind to you. You're . . ." one brow lifted appreciatively, "more lovely than you were—"

"—back then?" She finished his thought. "Thank you. I won't serve your ego by telling you what you must hear all the time: that you look great. The truth is, we've both grown a little older."

"Not wiser?"

She eyed him skeptically. "Age can't be helped. Wisdom takes some of us longer."

He clucked his chiding tongue against his teeth.

How long the train had been moving, Jenny had no idea, but as she glimpsed the last car disappearing past the glass doors, she whimpered a disappointed protest. It was hopeless, of course, yet she rushed to the door and threw her weight upon it. Icy wind gushed into the warmth of the terminal, and she stepped outside. She watched the 10:35 disappear with a sick feeling bubbling up in her stomach. Slumping then, she let out her breath and turned dejectedly back to the warmth of the indoors.

"Well, that's that," she mourned to herself. Her plans to buy the house had just gone back to square one.

The scuff of Everett's shoes as he caught up with her sent an irrational anger racing through her. How dare he be calm? This was his fault!

"You missed it," he observed with an incredibly pleasant grin.

Perhaps if she hadn't wasted so much of her life wanting him, Jenny would have taken this setback in her stride. But it was as if every frustrated dream of their courtship crashed down upon her at once. She whirled on him. Her brown eyes glistened with accusations that went back many more years than he could imagine.

"That's so clever of you, Everett!" she snapped. "I can see how you've come so far."

Stunned, Everett wanted to shake her for such unfairness. He watched her jerk about, saw her stride emphatically out the door and across the parking lot. He had half a mind to chalk the last five minutes up as a mistake and go about his own damned business. What a prickly little spitfire she'd become.

As Jenny reached for the door handle of her Volkswagen, she realized he had followed her.

"I've obviously ruined your day," he said, and braced his forearm against the window of her car.

"I don't know why you say that."

His laugh was irreverent. "If it were any more obvious, I'd need first aid." His hand clapped down over hers on the freezing chrome. His touch was hard, uncompromising. "Let me make amends."

To feel him actually touching her, when she'd spent so many years convincing herself that he was dead to her past, threw a sudden confusion into Jenny. His palm was warm and dry, and she felt moisture collecting on her own. Her mouth was so full of cotton she could hardly choke out the words.

"It's too far," she muttered.

Dragging her hand free, she began a convulsive search through her purse for her car keys. She found the key with frozen fingers and blindly attempted to put it into the lock.

His breath created hazy streams of vapor as he stood above her. He lifted the key from her fumbling hand, and his voice was deep and weighty. "I insist."

She gave him a sharp look. "And do you always get what you want, Everett Black?"

"Do I look as if I do?"

"You look like a tyrant."

Everett tipped back his head with a rousing laugh. "That's not tyranny. That's a windchill factor of fourteen below. Come on."

Dropping the key back into her palm by its ring, he promptly began ushering her toward the street. He indicated a sleek, rented Lincoln that had been freshly waxed. A film of slush was building up on the fenders.

He slipped a key in the lock and swung open the door on the passenger side.

Shivering, Jenny didn't protest as he slid across the seat first and started the engine with a growl. Warm air poured over her legs as she crawled in and slammed the door shut after her.

"Now, madame," he said, rubbing his hands with a lighthearted jauntiness Jenny guessed he didn't often indulge in, "where to? Do you need to call anyone? Your destination? Your husband? The police?"

She understood his question precisely. She should have expected it. The problem was, what doors would she be opening if she answered it?

The guardrails were going up; traffic was beginning to move again. Sitting quite still, Jenny listened for a moment to tires hissing on the slushy street. She figured he was nervous, too, but he had the advantage of having his hands upon the wheel.

Lacing her fingers on the top of her portfolio, she lowered her eyes to them when she answered. "I'm not married anymore, Everett."

Everett didn't reply.

"My husband was killed in Vietnam," she went on, since she'd said this much. "I have two boys. We live . . ." She sighed and looked out the window. "We moved away from the old house on Ferris Street. My mother lives with me, now that Martin's dead."

She paused, expecting him to recite all the clichés people said in the face of a tragedy: You're so young to be left alone; the worst casualties of war are those left at home.

Everett jabbed a thumb toward the interstate highway in the distance. "You were going into the city, I presume?"

Taken aback, feeling unexpectedly deprived, she almost wished she hadn't told him.

"I'm not married either," he said after a moment. "Nothing like your pain, though. Just a simple, civilized divorce that left me wanting to go somewhere and never be seen or heard of again."

"I'm sorry, Everett." At least *she* was sympathetic, she thought, piqued now.

"Why?" he said. "Marriage is a sacrificial ritual."

"That's a rather bitter remark coming from a man of such sensitivity."

"Man of sensitivity? I was the victim, dear."

She placed her portfolio comfortably beside her feet and crossed her legs. "Get your revenge," she suggested tartly. "Marry again."

His brows snapped down for a second, then he shook his head in a chuckle. "How wonderfully uncomplicated our sympathies are, Jenny."

She laughed, too, though she wasn't certain why. She let herself take the time to really study his face as he smiled—his white, even teeth, the sensual yet sensitive lines that framed his mouth, the thick fringe of his lashes and the creases fanning out from the corners of his eyes. His eyes had seen a lot and, by the looks of them, not all of it had been happy. He was, she had to admit, more irresistible than ever.

"And you shouldn't be sorry," he said dryly. "The divorce was my fault. It's a habit I've developed over the years—hurting people."

She doubted that. Growing warm, she unbuttoned her coat.

Gripping the steering wheel with one hand as he drove, Everett held her coat as she shrugged out of it. Her tweed skirt was lined, its slit reaching above the bend of her knee. As she moved he heard the discreet rustle of silk. Her perfume reached him when she twisted to place her coat on the backseat. Unable to tear his eyes away, though he knew he should, he glimpsed a swift flash of stockinged thigh and the fragile ecru lace of her panties.

Suddenly, unwillingly, he remembered running his tongue along that thigh. He jerked his gaze back to the highway. An unanticipated surge of desire pulsed through him now—a long-dormant ache rousing from its sleep, yawning, stretching, coming to life. At a loss as to what to do about it, he gripped the wheel until his knuckles crested white.

"No more hurting people?" she was asking. "Or no more marriage?"

"What? Oh, both."

"That keeps things conveniently neat."

"And you?"

She shrugged. "Marry again? Perhaps."

He looked from the highway to her and back. "Your excitement warms me about as much as this weather, my dear."

She deflected his implied disapproval. "He'd be a good father to the boys."

Expecting him to say that was a bad reason for marrying someone, she watched him concentrate on his driving.

"It's a virus," he said at length. "Everyone's going to marry someone."

She received his disenchantment. "At least you haven't come down with it. Count yourself lucky."

"I'm single. Not lucky."

An unwieldy silence lengthened in spite of Jenny's efforts. A far-reaching tapestry upon which their lives were stitched came together, then apart, then together, then . . . nothing. The ties of first love were like some invisible thread connecting two people. Whether it became hatred or love, one could never really hack it in two. She was certain he was wondering about her life. He had to be remembering the way he'd seduced her with kisses and sweet boyish wheedling. He had to be recalling how fervently she'd surrendered. She'd learned everything about love from him.

"Jenny?"

She started, aware now of the unwelcome feverishness washing over her. "What?"

"Was it . . ." He turned up one palm, as if he hated to look at her directly. "I don't know how to ask this. Was it ever a . . . problem with your husband? What we did?"

Once, in a fit of joining the physical fitness craze, Jenny had tried jogging. She hadn't been used to it. There had been moments when she was positive she was dying. She felt that same way now. Her breath seemed trapped in her body, strangling her; her blood pounded against her temples like the surf torturing the rocks. In the blurring skyline of Atlanta she saw Martin Howard's face.

"I never told him and he never asked. I always thought he knew, but . . ." She looked at Everett with ravaged honesty. "He loved me. Very much."

It was like admitting that the love of her marriage was one-sided. Quickly she said, "You didn't have children?"

He shook his head. "How old are yours?"

"Nine and ten."

"Oh."

She read his thoughts in the pensive way he set his jaw. "Jeffrey was Martin's child, Everett."

"I wasn't thinking that," he lied, his teeth clamping tightly.

Everett lied about children from habit. Whenever the subject arose, he said he'd had none from choice. In all the years that he and Ruth had been married, she'd never conceived. After a time he wondered if the fault was his. He adjusted to it, then he dismissed it. When the stormy times came, he'd been glad there weren't children to suffer through it with them. Yet, the feeling of loss had never subsided.

After a moment he smiled a thin, restrained smile. "Ten's a good age."

"No, it's not. It's awful."

"I see."

He didn't see, she knew. But he wasn't their father; it didn't matter.

Though it took some doing, Jenny gradually grew comfortable with Everett. He told her a bit about his project, which was doing nicely in Spain, about the Nobel prize that one of the scientists had been awarded. One of the first things she asked about was the interior decorating. Ruth, his ex-wife and a stock-holding member of his firm, had handled all that, he said, since she was rather good at interiors herself. Wasn't it funny how the two women he knew best were designers of one sort?

Jenny didn't find it at all amusing. She experienced a certain satisfaction when he told her that he'd brought in a firm to finish this last project, because of the divorce. She wondered if Ruth still held stock in his company, but she didn't ask. She told him about wanting to buy the house on Ferris Street instead. She described the shop she hoped to open for her mother, about her appointment with Alan Kendall at the bank. And she described her job with Pamela Chase. Occasionally he asked a question, but he offered no more of himself than she offered of herself.

"I'll go into the bank with you," he offered when he parked the car.

"No, no. That's not necessary."

"I'm sure it's not, but it never hurts to have a friend along. I'm an expert at asking for money."

Facing Alan Kendall with the meager proportions of her dream wasn't something Jenny looked forward to. But, ordering her own life, as lonely a business as that was, was something she was accustomed to doing single-handedly. Everett would be an intruder. Not an intruder, she corrected herself, an observer. She didn't want him seeing if she failed to get what she came after.

"You've done enough already," she said.

They both stiffened at the awkward double entendre.

Hurriedly she gathered up her portfolio. "I'd rather go by myself."

"What you mean is, your world's too fragile for an outsider."

Her brows drew together. "Don't put words in my mouth."

Leaning across her, grabbing the door handle before she could open it, Everett grinned maddeningly. "Darling, that's not what I'd like to do with your mouth."

She tried to look incensed. She even thrust his arm from over her lap. But his smile burned through her defenses like sunshine piercing through a mist. He could always wear her down, couldn't he?

"Oh, all right! You haven't changed very much, have you, Everett?"

Not until they were going through the smoked-glass doors did he answer her question. He opened a door for her and leaned back only enough for her to slip past him.

"I have changed, Jenny," he murmured. "Don't make that mistake."

Jenny was aware of her own small-town simplicity as she observed the worldliness lurking in his blue eyes.

How many women's hearts had this man broken besides hers? And, perhaps, Ruth's?

She smoothed the disorder of her hair that had resulted from the wind. "So have I," she said meaningfully. "And you shouldn't mistake *that*."

He only smiled and said he would read while she kept her appointment.

While Jenny climbed the dais of three steps to speak with Alan Kendall—she wondered if there was some significance in that queer number—she noted that Everett buried himself in a deep leather chair and flipped through a magazine. She guessed, however, that he was only pretending to read when she met his eyes over the banker's shoulder. What was he thinking? Was he comparing her to what she used to be? To the other women he knew?

The interview went badly from the beginning. She'd done business with Alan Kendall before. He was a distant friend of Ray Gerard, the man whom she would, in all probability, marry. Having "an understanding" with Ray Gerard didn't help her one iota with the banker, though.

"I can't do it," he said with a finality that left no alternatives.

Jenny crossed her legs and tried to look like Bartlett Street. She leaned forward across the glass-topped desk. She forced her voice steady.

"What you're telling me," she pinned him down, "is that my collateral is flimsy."

"Yes, Mrs. Howard."

"If my name were Mr. Howard, would I get the loan, flimsy collateral and all?"

He searched through his suit for his cigarette lighter. "You know I can't answer a question like that."

Jenny closed her portfolio and slipped the strap of

her purse over her shoulder. "You just did, Mr. Kendall."

Laughing, lighting himself a cigarette, holding it out from him while he snapped the lighter closed, Alan Kendall finally had the grace to shrug.

"You have a lot of responsibilities, Mrs. Howard. Even though the government assists you with the boys and your mother gets a small annuity, you're biting off a too-large bite here. Yes, if you were a man with a wife capable of working if she had to, I would seriously consider it. But I can't change policy, as much as I'd like to. Perhaps if you got me a solid cosigner . . ."

Rising, Jenny braced the tips of her fingers on the glass top of his desk. She pushed his ashtray nearer his cigarette, the ash of which was dangling precariously.

"Mr. Kendall," she said with the smiling, patient courtesy she reserved for her most difficult clients, "you are a chauvinist. I hope you never ask me to redecorate your house."

He returned her veiled criticism. "I'll be sure and remember that."

Jenny swept down the steps and walked angrily toward the expansion of glass that formed the front entrance.

Falling into step beside her, bracing his arm upon the door over her head, Everett recalled enough about her to let her fury burn itself out before he spoke. When he leaned upon the door, she stalked beneath the arch of his body.

"That makes me so damned mad!" she cried once she stepped out into the frigid wind and let it blow across her burning cheeks. "The nerve of that man! I'm a solvent creditor and he knows it. I've just never had a loan that big. He's—"

"You shouldn't get so upset, Jennifer." He stepped to the outside of the sidewalk. "It's not good for you."

His response was, surprisingly, disapproving. Jenny felt like she was supposed to beg his pardon for being disappointed because she'd had a dream die right in her hands. As he drove them back, she studied his profile until it whetted the blade of her control past the bearable point. What had once seemed his strength in her memories now seemed like an offensive obstinance chiseled out of pure granite.

"Nothing much seems to bother you, does it, Everett?" She peevishly broke the silence. "I envy you."

He threw her a look that bordered on accusation. "What's that supposed to mean?"

"Your control," she said reproachfully. She felt a hard pain in her stomach, as if a fist had battered it.

"Not so much control. Right now my life's going along pretty predictably."

"You don't seem to take chances." She should stop talking. "You don't laugh, you don't cry. Just what do you do, Everett?"

His eyes, when he riveted them upon her, were glowing with emotion. Jenny almost flinched when they scoured over her. She wondered if he realized how near to insulting his inspection was, flicking from her mouth to her breasts that way.

"I remember, that's what I do," he gritted. "Oh, hell, Jenny, I'm remembering right now. I'm remembering taking you down to the lake."

She took a quick breath of protest and shrank tightly against the door.

The tone of his voice grew gentle. "I'm remembering how trusting you were, Jenny. I'm remembering how I took off your clothes."

Jenny's head dropped downward as her hand came up to shield her face. "Don't. I shouldn't have said that."

"Then don't tell me what I am."

"I'm sorry." Her head came up. "But you're not responsible for me, now or then. No one made me do what I did."

"I don't like seeing you doing without things. Dammit, Jen, let me loan you the money for the house. I can afford it. Let me do that one thing for you."

Her affront blazed hotly. "Penance? At this late date? Oh, Everett!"

He looked at her as if to say, *I could slap your face.* Then he swore under his breath and concentrated on his driving. After a time, when they both invariably slipped into their memories of the other, their tempers gradually cooled. Everett glanced at Jenny's hands, laced tightly in her lap, her back outrageously stiff.

He laughed. "Come here."

She peered out the window.

"Come here."

Taking one of her hands, Everett dragged her closer on the seat beside him. He draped an arm about her shoulder and nestled her into the cozy hollow of his body. He looked down at the shining top of her head and leaned nearer. The smell of her hair was driving him mad.

"That wasn't so difficult, was it?"

She kept her face averted. "Yes."

His laughter was a beautiful, rich sound. He jutted his chin. "Back there. Reach into the backseat and get that list of properties out of my briefcase. Tell me where they are. I've forgotten the streets in my old hometown."

As Jenny bent over the front seat to fetch his briefcase, Everett again indulged himself in inspecting the trim lines of her legs, hoping to get a glimpse as delectable as before. This time he was disappointed.

Jenny balanced the pigskin case upon her knees and found the sheaf of papers stapled together.

"Hmm," she mused, putting on her glasses and glancing over the locations. "Some of these are very nice. The old Gaskin property is up for sale. I didn't know that. How long does it take to build one of these—"

When she stopped reading in mid-sentence, Everett turned slightly, his forehead questioning, and waited for her to finish.

Her jaw was loose. She made a strange strangling sound in her throat. Her gaze, when she drilled it into him, glittered with unshed tears. Jamming her hands together, she crumpled the sheets into a haphazard ball.

"Oh, you . . . you man!" she groaned. "You miserable, miserable—"

"What the hell . . . ?" he began.

But she had turned away from him, drooping like a bruised blossom, her face in her hands.

"What in blazes is the matter with you?" he stormed at her. "I'll swear, Jenny . . ."

Without lifting her head, she threw the wadded mass at him. "No wonder you wanted to go into the bank with me," she wept. "Don't ever ask me to trust you again."

There was no making sense of it. Everett closed his fist upon the papers and swung the big car onto the shoulder with an ominous crunch of gravel. The papers crinkled threateningly as he smoothed them out to see if he could find the cause of this confusion.

He drew his forefinger down the list of places listed with their penciled comments. He paused, then moved his fingertip back to one in particular. Feeling a prickle along his spine, he glanced over at the nape of her neck as it bent, the hunch of her shoulders as they shook. The fifth property on the list was a large, three-story house on Ferris Street. "House removal necessary," the marginal comment said. It was the house where he had fidgeted at the dining table beneath the hawk eye of her father, the house where they had parked in his old Chevy and held each other, the house where he'd gone through agony trying to kiss her beneath a porch light as big as the moon. Lord help him, it was *her* house.

Chapter Two

Jenny's mistake didn't chide her with mild recriminations; it thundered and howled and made her head shatter with self-disgust. She shrank against the door of Everett's car and dragged her coat about herself in a gesture of abject despair. She'd known better than to let this happen. She'd let down her barriers enough to trust this man again. Only a fool went back to the same old fire and stuck his hand into the flame.

As if it had somehow set out to ruin him, Everett scowled at the list of properties in his hand. Frowning, he placed it upon his knee and folded it in half and smoothed it again.

"Jenny," he said, hating the uncertainty that made him feel like a boy needing to justify himself, "this isn't how it looks."

Jenny shivered. She watched him handling the list. His nails, when he sharpened the crease, were neat and well tended, like his carefully chosen words. Everett

Black had become quite guarded with the passing of years.

"Tell me how it is, then," she said acridly. "Tell me how I have any chance at all against money like your . . . foundation, or whatever it is that you are."

"I'm only a consultant and it's a firm, not a foundation. You're overreacting, Jenny. You know I didn't plan this."

"Overreacting?" Her brows arched derisively. "That's so chauvinistic, Everett. You men amaze me, you really do. First Alan Kendall shoots me down and calls it policy. Now you, with some humane cause I can't even put a name on. And you have the nerve to say that to me. If a man defends himself you call it corporate aggression. If a woman does it you say she's overreacting."

Everett grinned at her doggedness.

"In the first place, my dear," he shook his head, "if I were going to shoot you down, it wouldn't be for a humane cause. And I'm not a chauvinist."

"A chauvinist is identifiable in that he twists everything around to have a sexual connotation."

Laughing, Everett extended a lean leg and adjusted the crease of his trousers.

"Well, maybe I'm half chauvinist. I've been called worse by far less-informed individuals. Anyway, Jenny, it isn't me who's buying the property. It's the people I represent. And I don't have to present this particular property and you know it. There're others on that list that'll probably do equally well."

She hadn't expected him to be nice about it. She toyed with a curl at her temple and lowered her eyes.

"But you'll want it," she said, weakening. "It'll be perfect for you—the location, the price, everything. Esther Simmons is trying to put First Mark Realty on the map with the sale of this house. It'll be a steal. If you tell her it's for a humane cause, she'll probably lower the price again."

"If you use the word *humane* one more time," he said, laughter buried deep in his chest as he glanced back at the lanes of oncoming traffic, "I'm going to do something quite scandalous."

"You, the dignified financier, do something scandalous?" she mocked, but with less defensiveness. "You mean like not walk me to my car?"

He nosed the big car back onto the highway and concentrated on his driving. After a moment he observed her still-adamant posture, her tightly crossed knees, her inflexible thighs.

"I was thinking more of taking you out in the center lane of the interstate and kissing you," he chuckled.

"That wouldn't be scandalous." Jenny's grimace, halfway between a smile and a frown, languished. "That would be suicide."

In that respect, she thought, Everett hadn't changed a great deal over the years. He still had that disarming streak of pacifism he could call up when it suited him. Even when they'd broken up, it had been so civilized. "We shouldn't tie ourselves down to one person just yet," he'd said. She could picture him getting his divorce and cordially shaking Ruth's hand good-bye. Or perhaps he'd kissed her and wished her the best of everything. Did this man ever lose his head like everyone else? Like she did? Or was that invincible self-control in his blood now?

She leaned her forehead against the cold window and stared at the spires of grass blurring beside the road. Everett was right, actually; she was overreacting. But dreams had a way of hurting when they died. Her dream of spending her life with him—being the center of his world—had hurt most of all. Until he had reappeared today, she'd almost come to terms with a life without dreams. She accepted each day as being a series of exacting roles into which she stepped. She separated her own personal wishes from what she was doing, reached the end of the day exhausted, and fell asleep before she could feel cheated. Why had he come back, damn him? Why must she be reminded of the one thing she didn't have, would never have?

Not until she felt the engine snarling to a stop did Jenny drift back to where she was. Lifting her head, the first thing she saw was the cold, shimmering skeleton of the willow tree a block away. Ice encrusted, it seemed gloomily symbolic of her whole day, her whole life.

"What are you doing, Everett?" She drew herself up. "Returning to the scene of the crime? Pouring salt in the wound?"

"That's never been one of my turn-ons in life, salting wounds. But then," he deflected her criticism with a wry deprecation, "if you talked to my ex-wife, she might say differently."

She was surprised at this evidence of pain. At least she'd had the consolation, when Martin was killed, that something outside herself was to blame. Everett faulted himself. For one wild, insane moment she wanted to take his handsome face between her hands. *Why didn't you marry me?* she wanted to cry. *I wouldn't have hurt you.*

"What?" he asked, thinking she had started to speak.

She blinked rapidly. Had she betrayed her own thoughts?

"Never mind," she mumbled.

Shrugging, Everett squinted at the red brick house where Jenny had grown up. The paint on the shutters was peeling, and the mortar in the chimneys had crumbled with age. Some of the screens dangled unevenly. The veranda on the west side demanded a new foundation, and the outbuildings shivered with neglect. The whole property seemed to be settling into irreversible decay, yearning for a compassionate, merciful hand to put it out of its misery.

He twisted around to warn her of the vastness of her undertaking if she bought this house. From the corner of his eye he saw her hand discreetly curved about her eyes, trying to blot away the dampness without his seeing. Unexpectedly, for it had been a long time since he'd been emotionally involved with a woman, he was conscious of a need to comfort her.

Quickly he averted his head. He made a ceremony out of pocketing his keys. He tactfully reached for his briefcase on the backseat and for some minutes pretended to shuffle through its contents. When he glanced up, her composure was once more intact.

"Everyone is looking at this place today," she observed with painstaking interest. "Esther must have run another ad."

"You're a professional pessimist." Everett reached for his door. "You will be nice, won't you, Jenny, and not embarrass me while we look at this house?"

She snapped back with the barbed riposte he was hoping for. "I've seen this house before, you know."

"Not with me, you haven't."

The regret that passed across Jenny's face was a veil, misty and ghostlike. "Yes, I have," she choked.

Sighing remorsefully, Everett squeezed his eyes shut and pinched the bridge of his nose. He ruefully shook his head. "I'm saying all the wrong things to you, aren't I?" Gently then, he coaxed her head up. "Jenny?"

The look they shared was one of mutual misgiving. It reached far, far into the past with a realism neither of them could cope with. With a resilience Everett had forgotten she was capable of, Jenny pulled herself upright. She squared her shoulders like a veteran soldier dedicated to victory, no matter what.

"Well, that doesn't matter," she said a little too briskly. "Now that we're here, we might as well go in and visit the past. We'll exorcise our memories with Esther Simmons."

The January wind bit viciously as they rushed across the crunching dead grass, up the rickety steps, and through the front door with its pane of stained glass. Once inside, Everett slammed the door shut and stamped his feet, rubbing his palms together. Jenny blew on her fingertips, then hugged herself, laughing at him as he pinched the half-frozen lobes of his ears.

"This is really a dumb thing to do," she said.

Everett picked up on her fragile lightheartedness. "It won't be my first dumb thing, lady. Let's find your friend, Miss Simmons, and see how she reacts to humane causes."

"She's not my friend." Jenny smiled as Esther Simmons popped into view at the head of the curved stairway. She added in a whisper, "I've only talked with her once on the telephone."

"Hello, hello!" Esther smoothed the waist of a stunningly unbecoming skirt. She stood at the head of the stairs like a plump housewife in a painting, beaming down at them as if they were relatives coming in for the holidays. "Sorry to have missed you when you came in, but my latest ad has worked miracles. Everyone's braved this terrible weather." She descended two steps. "I'm Esther Simmons, Mr. . . . ahh—"

"Everett Black."

"Oh, yes, Mr. Black. I received a card just yesterday from your office, saying to expect you. I'm so glad to meet you. And you, too, Mrs. Black."

The mistake was so sudden, so intensely personal, a

full five seconds passed before Jenny could collect her poise. Esther motioned them to follow her, then went back upstairs as if it were not possible that they wouldn't come. Jenny gripped the banister. She reached one hand outward as if she could stop the woman.

"Oh," she protested, "but we—"

"—will be happy to see the house."

Everett cut Jenny off and pushed her up the step. With a grin that Jenny considered to be only slightly less than obscene, he prodded her upward. He steered her down the hallway in the wake of the bustling realty agent like a principal herding a delinquent student to his office.

The sturdiness of Everett's wool suit didn't prevent Jenny's elbow from finding his rib with a well-placed jab. Her small vengeance was truly hurtful, and he drew in a sharp breath. Struggling to keep from attracting the attention of Miss Simmons and at the same time attempting to protect himself, Everett trapped Jenny's arm tightly between them.

"Vicious little rowdy, aren't you?" he chuckled. He drew her into the curve of his side so that her whole body was imprisoned securely against the contours of his own. "You promised you wouldn't embarrass me."

"I didn't promise you anything. Tell her the truth, you . . . you fraud!"

"Aw, let her think we're the perfect couple. Don't you think we look like a match made in heaven?"

"I thought you'd sworn off marriage."

"I have, totally. But it makes her happy. It's a harmless enough mistake."

No mistake was harmless, Jenny thought, and marriage to Everett was never a thing to joke about. She twisted her shoulder and wriggled free of him. At that exact moment Esther Simmons turned back to point out an unusual Romanesque mosaic window that Jenny had grown bored with years ago. Jenny didn't even glance at it. Like a practiced mime, she reversed her pout and curved a ludicrous smile across her face.

"It's quite lovely," she cooed. "I've always admired stained glass."

The muffled coughing from Everett sent pink abashment spreading over her cheeks.

Esther frowningly continued her spiel. "If you're interested in the house for its residential charms, it's perfect for the growing family. Do you have children?"

"Yes," Jenny blurted automatically.

"No," Everett replied at the same moment.

Confusion flickered across Esther's features. She had one unwavering rule: Never become involved with people's personal lives. Her memorized selling points rippled out of her mouth like an agitated, computerized printout.

The joke ended awkwardly. As Esther rushed on to describe this and that, Everett stuffed his hands into his pockets and broodingly pretended to inspect the ceiling. Beneath lowered lids Jenny watched him go over the floor plan. She was certain he saw none of it. The mention of children had really bothered him, hadn't it? Was Everett disappointed that he wasn't a father? Did he cherish visions of passing down a legacy through his sons?

Time dragged as Esther showed them things Jenny had grown up with. Once they were downstairs she watched people callously tracking mud on the floors, slamming doors, and kicking at the edges of the rugs. Everything in the house held a memory for her, and it grieved her to see them trodden beneath people's feet or bumped aside with their shoulders. Now she wished that she'd insisted Everett take her straight home.

"Shabby upkeep, if you ask me," observed a man in

a yellow Windbreaker whose trousers were three inches too short. "Seems like people would take more pride in appearances."

One woman who had to have borne a half-dozen children rubbed her finger over the doorjamb. "That paint is scrubbed down to the base coat," she criticized. She turned to Jenny as if she should sympathize. "You have to watch these realtors," she confided behind her hand. "They'll pawn any old piece of junk off on a person. Who'd want this drafty barn, anyway?"

"You couldn't pay me enough to live here, Jack," a wife whispered to her husband. "There's no telling what a person could catch."

Overwhelmed, feeling they were all looking at her with mounting suspicion, as if it were her fault the doorjambs had been scrubbed too many times or her neglect that the calking was cracked, Jenny jumped when a man behind her spoke.

"Run-down old shed," he grumbled. "I'd have a bulldozer out here in a week."

Jenny glanced about for Everett, then hurried toward the back door. Her heels clicked a frustrated staccato upon the cracked linoleum of the kitchen. She rushed out through the storeroom and onto the back porch.

The cold wind hurt when she stepped outside, but at least it was real and unpretentious. Slumping back against the bricks, she abruptly found herself unable to hold back the tears that had waited all day to be wept.

"Why did I come here?" she groaned to herself. "Why did I let him bring me here?"

Beside her the screen door creaked open and slammed gently shut. Everett, she thought. She didn't want to see anyone, particularly him. She twisted her face away and tried to repair her face before he could catch her crying.

"My, but the wind is really raw out here," she

mumbled and removed her glasses. She cleaned them with a wadded tissue from her pocket and went through a much-too-tedious process of replacing them upon her nose.

Everett stood observing her ritual with reserved, masculine silence. Tucking his hands in the warm niche beneath his arms, he smiled. Still he remained silent.

"This is really unnatural weather for Atlanta, you know." Jenny couldn't stop chattering. *"You know? What am I saying? Of course you know. I keep forgetting you grew up here."* She tossed out an improvident gesture. "You probably know more about—"

Stepping directly before her, capturing her uplifted hand, Everett closed it firmly into his. He gazed down at her with a mixture of conflicting emotions.

"It's all right to cry," he said solemnly.

She choked a wracking sob. "I'm not crying."

Smiling, shushing her as she had so often shushed her own heartbroken children, he folded his arms about her and drew her head to the hard pillow of his shoulder. He rocked her back and forth against him.

His tenderness completely devastated her.

"It's such a fight all the time," she wept. "To get one inch. I fight with the Army for the sake of Martin's sons. I fight with the bank. I fight just to get a credit card in my own name. I fight to prove I've paid bills I've already paid. And now I'm fighting strangers because of things they have a perfect right to say."

"People love to have opinions, Jenny," he murmured against the crown of her head. "Don't let some old Transmanian warthog get your goat."

Half crying, half laughing, Jenny wriggled in his arms. Her snuffling dwindled until it was more of a distorted hiccough.

"You're mixing your metaphors," she sniffed against the comfort of his suit. "Bad form, Miss Pruitt would say."

Chuckling, Everett continued to hold her. Against the curve of her forehead he said, "I thought you were going to tell me there weren't any warthogs in Transmania."

She tipped her face, innocence dewy in her eyes, the lenses of her glasses a mass of smudges. "Isn't there?"

Suddenly, tears still sparkling, she laughed, an uninhibited mirth that pleased him immensely. His dark head touched hers as his laughter blended melodically. Holding her side, she leaned into him for support. And, accepting it, he chuckled, not at the humor but because it was so right to hold her.

Still smiling, he hesitantly lifted his hands to her glasses. He drew off one earpiece rather clumsily, and the other hung in her tangle of curls. She winced and he grimaced. Between them they succeeded in removing the glasses, and he slipped them into the outside pocket of his jacket without comment.

The laughter gone, they both stilled. They were thinking of where they were now, and Jenny felt the cold air up her skirt, along her spine. The danger of the moment ticked like a time bomb lying at their feet. When Everett made no move to defuse it, she willed herself to step away from him. She couldn't move. He bent his head and leaned, ever so slightly, until his lips brushed her cheek—a wispy suggestion of a kiss.

"You shouldn't . . ." she choked.

"Shouldn't what?" he said, doing it again.

"That."

"This?" he muttered at the same time that he took the necessary step to pin her to the wall at her back. His dark head bent with infinite slowness. His lips, parting, traveled the line of her jaw. His breath was warm and captivating.

"Oh, Jenny," he groaned and suddenly buried his face into the soft curls behind her ear.

For a split second Jenny was under the willow tree again—young, innocent, hurting with the old familiar pain. When the coldness began to sharpen her senses and her nostrils filled with the crisp, clean smell of his hair, she knew, and Everett knew, what would happen. They were drawn by the same magnet of the past, and both their heads rose. She watched him moisten his lips without breaking the spell of his gaze. She saw her own reflection in the blue of his eyes.

"I have to kiss you," he whispered, his brows insistent.

"I know."

In a sustained motion, realizing everything that was happening and not being able to stop any of it, their heads tilted slightly and, with painstaking care, slowly came together.

"I didn't plan—" His eyes were closing.

"Neither did—"

Their mouths and noses fit perfectly together.

Everett's exploration of what he had forgotten about her was timorous at first. Jenny wasn't certain how he unbuttoned her coat to shape his hands about her ribs. She only knew that as he flicked his tongue against her teeth, as he parted her lips with his and drew a questioning breath against them, she was where she wanted to be. She wouldn't think about the past or the future, only his hand moving to the base of her spine and drawing her body into the strong, powerful angles below his waist.

"Everett?"

She whimpered into the kiss, not expecting to feel

the swift rush of heat that flooded through her. Frightened, uncertain, she staggered from the violence of it.

"Ev—"

The moment she slumped, Everett's arms tightened about her with the fierceness of a sprung trap. His mouth twisted hard, as if he were driven unexpectedly to search out every intimate memory, every taste. Jenny met him with a feverishness she'd never experienced before. Everything, even the coldness surrounding them, burst into a torrent of flames: a burning, a searing, a desperate straining to be closer, which was not possible, for they were already touching everywhere. She felt herself sinking into the heat of his desire, and she thought, *I am lost, I am lost.*

Everett had always been a man to trust his inner instincts. He always knew exactly where he was going and what he wanted. Yet, when it came to women, even the one he held in his arms with an arousal more shattering than he'd known in years—especially this one—he didn't trust himself. The pain he'd suffered with Ruth hacked through his senses.

Struck with his own failures, he jerked himself upright. He removed Jenny's hands from the back of his head; brows blunted, as if he weren't certain just where he was, he stepped away.

Jenny blinked at him in weak confusion. Her lips were still bruised to a rose color. Her eyes were still glazed in response. She didn't understand his reaction except that it must, in some ghastly, terrible way, be something she'd done. What? What was the matter with her that he could reject her once and come back into her life and do it again? *What mistake was she repeating?* Her head moved from side to side in dazed bewilderment.

"It's not you," he said quickly. "It's not you."

She knew he was lying.

In the space of a heartbeat Everett watched an opaque shroud of anguish drop over Jenny's features. It was the same self-discipline he'd witnessed in the car, yet different. She smiled, not a smile but a shield against everything outside herself. Her guard was so perfect, he knew penetrating it was hopeless.

"Jenny—"

"I'm all right now," she said coolly. "Could you take me back to my car, please?"

Not once did they speak during the drive back to the train terminal. A dozen apologies writhed inside Everett's head; he said none of them. *Best leave it alone, you idiot,* a voice cautioned him. *Remember Ruth.*

"If you . . ." he managed to say as she swung out the door without waiting for him to help her.

He reached across the space of the seat as if he would grasp her coat and physically prevent her from leaving.

"If you're ever back in town," she began the habitual courtesy that Southern women were born with, a tact that meant nothing, "well . . ."

She didn't finish speaking, and she didn't look back. She walked through the bitter cold with a strength that made him want to lean his head upon the steering wheel and weep. But, of course, men didn't cry. He watched, lips tightly compressed, until he couldn't see her bright little Vokswagen any longer. Then, knowing it was something he wanted to do, something he *must* do, he got out of the car and walked back into the terminal.

His whole life had changed since he'd been here only hours before. He stepped to the same telephone booth, checked for a number, and dialed.

"First Mark Realty," came a lusterless voice.

"Yes, this is Everett Black. I called ahead because this is important. The property you list on Ferris Street is sold. I'll be there in fifteen minutes to give you a check."

He stared at the phone for a moment after he hung up. Then, squaring his shoulders, smiling somewhere inside himself because he had bought it for her and it made life tolerable again, he leaned against the glass door. He walked, without feeling the cold, back to his car.

Chapter Three

Jenny's mother was a proud, admirable woman whose pinnacle of extravagance was viewing a situation comedy on television. She was well known in the neighborhood for being particular about the habits of her two grandsons. No one ever saw the Howard boys tipping over garbage cans, it was said, or turning up the stereo so loudly the vibrations shook all the windows on the block. She kept a meticulous lawn, attended church faithfully, and believed rigorously in the family structure. Her one unfulfilled longing was to see Jenny happily married to Ray Gerard.

Tonight Mildred invariably seated Jenny beside her prospective son-in-law. She placed Jeffrey and Stephen at her own right and left—for strategic reasons, Jenny supposed, to give the "widowed daughter" the opportunity of devoting herself entirely to the "eligible bachelor." And Mildred expressly forbade Jeffrey to speak of yesterday's difficulty with the middle-school principal.

"Be on your best behavior tonight, Jeffrey Howard," Jenny overheard her mother's last-minute·instructions, "or you'll have me to deal with in the morning. There'll be no rudeness to Ray Gerard like last time."

"Ray isn't my daddy," Jeffrey replied with a ten-year-old petulance that made Jenny wonder if he would ever accept Ray. "He can't make me join the boys' club."

"He may very well be your father someday."

"Mother'll never marry Ray."

"I wouldn't count on that."

"I'll leave home, then."

"Don't be silly. Where would you go?"

"I don't know. Somewhere. I'll move over to John Schneider's."

It wasn't that Mildred was an overbearing woman, Jenny decided. She only had a closed mind upon one particular subject: Ray Gerard. The well-to-do banker, Mildred had observed many times, was Jenny's way out.

"Way out of what, Mother?" Jenny's reply was always the same. "I have what I want—a job, my children, and my private bag of tricks for remaining reasonably sane. What more do I need?"

"Do you think that's all there is to life?" Mildred argued. She wanted something for her daughter besides the daily grind of hard work she'd always had. "Eating, drinking, and wearing?"

"There're worse things."

"Ray Gerard can make you financially independent."

"A woman of leisure, Mother? Really."

"He can take you places, Jennifer. He can keep you from being alone. He can be a father to your children."

In her mind Jenny admitted the boys' need of a father. But was Ray the father for Jeffrey? And what of her own need for a husband? She'd never been able to fantasize romantically about Ray Gerard and herself. He wasn't bad-looking with his height and his sophisticated silver temples, his Christian Dior suits and his black Audi. He wasn't badly educated—a Harvard degree that had prepared him for the presidency of his own bank. He possessed that elegant, understated charisma in which the rich abound. Ray Gerard was everything any woman would want, and most of them did. Why didn't she?

"Ray Gerard is in love with you," Mildred reminded her.

"But I don't love him."

"I learned to love your father. It took awhile, but I learned."

Jenny could remember the hard years of learning to love. "I guess I'm naive, Mother. I've always wanted the little things—the sweet words and the empathy. The good books and the music. Is it silly to dream of a jug of wine and a summer day?"

Nearly six decades of disillusionment made Mildred shake her head. "Lovers talk about books and music and have empathy. Husbands make house payments and figure the income tax and see that the yard gets mowed."

"Well, I don't have the nerve to take a lover. So where does that leave me?"

"With two boys who need a father and a yard that needs mowing."

It always ended that way. Tonight, still numb from her earlier encounter with Everett, carefully hidden behind the civilized tinkle of bone china and silver, Jenny tried not to call attention to herself. She smoothed her napkin over a wool plaid skirt she'd gone to considerable expense and time to make. Casting a sidelong glance at the man whose merits Mildred lauded so highly, she pictured herself having dinner with Ray every evening in their own home. Then she envisioned a lifelong conflict between Ray and Jeffrey.

Disheartened, she laid down her fork.

Up until several hours ago her ears had been deaf to her mother's constant litany of marrying again. But so much had happened today: She hadn't been able to buy her house; Everett had reappeared in her life, and he had rejected her even more painfully than before.

She felt the compulsion to do something radical and decisive. She couldn't keep drifting through life at the mercy of silly, mushy dreams of a Prince Charming–husband–lover. And she couldn't fall back into the trap of thinking about Everett Black in terms of what might have been!

Tonight, Jenny told herself as the chime of the doorbell jolted her moody eyes into focus, she would be practical. Tonight when Ray asked her to marry him—as he always did—she would talk to him about Jeffrey. Perhaps she could bring herself to say yes, she would marry him. Then the future would fill the vacuum of the past. Her open wounds from Everett would heal. Wouldn't they?

"I'll get it!" yelled Stephen. Towheaded, lovably rowdy, he scrambled from the table and darted toward the front door, which was partially visible from the cubbyhole of a dining room. "It's probably for me."

"Sit down, Stephen." Jenny calmly rose to follow him. "Finish your dinner."

But Stephen was already jerking open the heavy door when his mother's words got out of her mouth. A gust of cold air whistled through the room. Automatically the boy peered around the tall, well-dressed man to the Lincoln parked in front of the house. His boyish aplomb suddenly drooped.

"Oh, hello," he said with an uncertain courtesy. "Did you come to see Ray?"

If Everett's appearance only hours before had undone Jenny, seeing him now on her front porch devastated her completely. It was like reaching for a step and not finding one. She shrank backward, fingers hovering at her throat, her thoughts spinning in a wild, mad flurry.

Everett's look clung to hers for a moment—nothing like her confused one, nothing like the one that had been on his face after he'd kissed her. She received the impression that he'd like her indulgence for appearing so unexpectedly on her doorstep, but if she didn't give it, he wouldn't turn around and go away. He stepped resolutely through the door and closed it without waiting to be invited.

"Of course not, Stephen," she blurted. "This is Mr. Black. He came to . . ." She dwindled down to nothing. She had no idea why he'd come.

Everett gave Stephen one of his flashing, persuasive smiles. "You must be . . ." He drew out the word and extended his hand to the boy. "Now, don't tell me. . . ."

Stephen's blustering congeniality eroded slightly. Twisting the tail of his shirt with one hand, he tentatively accepted the stranger's handshake with the other.

"You must be Stephen," Everett finished. "Well, Stephen, I went to school with your mother when I was just about your age. She was very bad in math as I remember, but excellent in poetry."

Time is like a fashionable host, / That slightly shakes his parting guest by the hand, Jenny recalled with a sharp little breath.

The sound of her mother's chair scraping back from the table made her start.

"Why, you're . . . Everett Black," Mildred said wonderingly as she approached. She remembered him wearing faded jeans, worn-out sneakers, and a baseball cap, knocking at the back door. Immediately she drew herself up, demanding with her aloofness what he meant by returning to their lives after all these years.

Everett's smile eroded a fraction. "Like the bad penny, I'm afraid, Mrs. Stephenson."

"How's your mother, Everett? Your sister?" Mildred knew better than to ask about his father and brother. Phillip Black had run off with his secretary when Everett was seventeen years old. No one knew much about Saul. After several marriages he'd moved on.

"Mother's still in the classroom. Always will be, I guess. Claire is married now, doing the motherhood thing."

In the tension of the moment Jenny almost forgot Ray. He was rising from the table and blotting his lips meticulously. He gave a slight adjustment to the vest of his suit, buttoned his suitcoat, then moved behind her right shoulder as if he were about to be photographed.

'I don't believe I've had the pleasure," he said with suspicious restraint. "I'm Ray Gerard."

"Ahh . . . Everett!" Jenny spoke his name like the dazed announcer of a boxing match. *And in this corner, ladies and gentlemen . . .*

Then, on the chance that the rippling undercurrents would disappear with the more mundane ceremony of introductions, she drew Ray beside her.

"How rude of me. Everett, I'd like you to meet Mr. Ray Gerard. Ray, this is Everett Black, an old friend of mine from high school." She frowned. Shouldn't she have introduced Everett to Ray?

The two men exchanged a spare handshake.

Everett appeared much less interested in Ray than the blond-haired boy who was keeping himself distant from the rest. "Only an older friend getting older," he replied as if he didn't hear his own words.

He lifted slightly venturing eyebrows and smiled at Jeffrey Howard. Jeffrey's eyes burned with belligerent wonder as he returned Everett's swift assessment.

Seeing the exchange, Jenny suffered horrors of Jeffrey embarrassing her as he had with Ray a number of times. "Ray's a dear friend of our family," she chattered brightly. "He's also the president of People's State Bank. It's new. You probably don't know where it is."

Everett shook his head. The confrontation between Jeffrey and himself was like a small piece of side action that managed, by its very intensity, to claim center stage. "No, I'm sorry."

Jenny slumped slightly. How dare Everett come here unannounced like this? How could she explain him to Ray without arousing his curiosity? *What was going on between Everett and her son?*

"Well," she explained uselessly, "it's on the east side of town. That section of town is really growing."

The silence was laced with strained, shadowy courtesy. No one made a move to penetrate it. Jenny grew so nervous she stepped back, nearer Jeffrey, and motioned him to stand in front of her. She rested her hands upon his shoulders. He reached past her chin.

"This is my older son," she said.

"So you're Jeffrey." Everett considered the boy's intelligent, sensitive, and, at the moment, thoroughly distrustful features. Jenny possessed an exceptional boy in her older son, he guessed. A real handful.

Somehow Jeffrey had managed to be born with the best characteristics of both his parents. At ten, his wavy blond hair framed a face as pretty as a girl's. It wasn't yet chiseled with masculinity. This physical beauty, coupled with an extraordinarily quick mind, created many more problems for him than his happy-go-lucky brother had. Stephen possessed the more squarish, clear features of his father and tended to float through life in a constant state of contented bliss. Jeffrey's temper was closer to the surface. His present difficulty at school stemmed from being taunted as "pretty boy."

"Yessir," he said rather tensely. "How'd you know my name?"

Everett lifted a shoulder. "Your mother told me."

It had never occurred to Jeffrey that his mother had an interest in any man besides Ray Gerard. If she'd told this strange person his name, she'd surely told that the principal had suspended him from school for fighting. With an instinct he didn't clearly understand, he came back with the only counterattack he knew.

"Mother and Ray are getting married," he announced, letting the words fall with intentional weight.

Everett's face didn't alter a fraction, though he heard a slight gasp from Mildred and caught the sudden tightening of Jenny's fingers on her son's shoulders.

"I'm sure my marriage plans are of little interest to Mr. Black, Jeffrey." Jenny was cutting off the circulation in one of Jeffrey's arms.

"She told me she might," Everett replied blandly. "Lucky for you, Jeffrey, having a banker in the family. Right?"

Jeffrey's testy poise frayed. Having a banker in the family was the last thing he wanted. He squirmed from the increasing punishment of his mother's hands and lifted one throbbing shoulder.

"Oh, yeah . . . well, I guess so."

Jenny could have shaken Jeffrey until his ears rang.

"Perhaps you'd better do your homework now, Jeffrey, if you've finished eating."

Mildred's Southern hospitality was unwavering, no matter what she thought of Everett personally. "Would you let me fix you a plate, Everett?" she invited.

"Oh, no, thank you, Mrs. Stephenson. Really."

"Does this mean you won't be taking us to the mall?" Jeffrey glanced at the two adult men as if they were complicating his life unnecessarily.

"If the homework gets done"—Jenny hesitated in the way of mothers when they were trapped in front of guests—"perhaps one round of Pac-Man. No more."

Ray positioned himself nearer Jenny's obstinate son. "Better do as your mother says," he suggested with a deep-throated military tone.

Without replying, Jeffrey flicked a hostile gaze over Ray. He returned to Everett. "You play Pac-Man?"

"Sometimes," Everett replied. "I may not be as good as your friend Ray, though."

"Ray doesn't play," Jeffrey informed tactlessly, quite willing to forget Ray now. "What's your high score?"

"Jeffrey!"

"That's all right, Jenny." Feeling rather on trial as Jeffrey made lightning comparisons between Ray and himself, Everett answered, "About three hundred thousand. What's yours?"

Jeffrey's jaw hung loose. "Gaaa . . ."

An instant camaraderie replaced Jeffrey's standoffishness. He threw a triumphant glance at Stephen, as if he'd at last met the man who satisfied his high standards of accomplishments. He allowed the faintest grin to curve up his lips.

"Not nearly that," he admitted, and hooked a thumb in the belt loop of his jeans.

"It takes a little time."

Jeffrey's eagerness to get to know Everett better

prompted him to step nearer. "I do pretty well," he said, "until I reach the fourth key."

Everett laughed. He clapped a friendly hand on the boy's shoulder. "When those little monsters stop turning blue it really gets tough, doesn't it?"

"Have you tried Ms. Pac-Man? It's a killer."

If Ray hadn't shifted his weight and pointedly begun scowling, Everett might have let Jeffrey indulge in his need to converse with a man he identified with. But he was the intruder here. Complicating Jenny's life wasn't something he planned to do. He ran his fingers through his hair and wondered how he was ever going to tell her he'd bought the house on Ferris Street for her.

Before Jenny could express her surprise or her gratitude that Jeffrey had finally shown interest in an adult, Mildred took the matter wonderfully out of her hands. She suggested that the boys retire to their rooms.

"Aw, Grandma," they chimed, as though on cue.

"Now," she clipped with devoted firmness, "or it's bread and water for a week."

Stephen departed with a wag of his head and an indecipherable string of moans and groans. More subdued, Jeffrey cast a thoughtful glance back at Everett.

Everett grinned. "Tough life, ain't it?"

Jeffrey flashed him a rare smile and followed the urging hand of his grandmother.

During her mother's absence, Jenny's attempt to strike some note of geniality between the two men varied from the morose to the disgusting. Fortunately, Ray was a master at talking about himself. Once Everett steered the conversation to the banker's work, Jenny saw her chance to escape. She mumbled something about after-dinner coffee and jumped up from her seat.

"I'll be back in a minute," she said, just as the prime interest rate launched Ray on a lengthy discourse.

Everett, pretending avid interest, rose before Jenny reached the door. "Excuse me a minute, Ray," he called over his shoulder.

Stepping over to Jenny, he said loudly enough for Ray's benefit, "I told my telephone service where I'd be. I hope you don't mind." Then, very softly, coaxing hoarse in his voice, "I have to see you, Jenny. Alone."

"It's the fault of the oil companies," Ray was saying. "Why, I could list . . ."

Caught totally off guard, unable to reconcile Everett's demand to see her with his earlier reaction to their kiss, Jenny rubbed distractedly at the space between her brows.

"Of course I don't mind." She heard her words coming with gracious courtesy. "My telephone is your telephone." Then, in a barbed whisper: "You have your nerve asking me that."

"The sale of wheat to the Russians didn't help any, either," said Everett, adroitly maintaining his conversation with Ray. "By the way, Jenny," he continued, to allay Ray's suspicion, "you left these when we had our . . . meeting."

He withdrew her eyeglasses from a pocket and, grinning at her surprise, tapped them upon the side of his jaw.

Jenny, blinking twice, found it increasingly difficult to think clearly. She took in a breath, held it, then said in a small, high voice, "Why, thank you. I hadn't even missed them."

She reached for the glasses, but Everett shifted them to his other hand.

"Meet me," he persisted inaudibly.

"No!"

Ray had to be picking up on the strange lulls in the conversation, Jenny told herself. Couldn't he take one look at her and tell that her legs would hardly hold her up? That her color was so abnormally high she could feel it scorching her earlobes?

Everett demanded she look at him. "We have to talk."

"We talked already."

Behind them, Ray stirred as if he were about to rise.

Everett glanced toward him, then swiftly back to Jenny. "Dammit, Jenny!" he muttered. Louder, he said, "It's good to see your family again, Jenny. I don't suppose you've kept up with Bob Crandall?"

She struggled to recapture the devastation she'd felt when he'd released her and taken that fateful step backward. "Ahh . . . yes," she said stiffly. "I mean, no, I haven't seen Bob Crandall in years. I hear things from time to time, of course." She sighed. "I think his wife died."

Frowning, Everett sighed too.

She couldn't take much more of this. "I'll get the coffee," she blurted. "In the meantime, feel free to"—she made a helpless gesture "—to do anything."

Behind them, Ray was strolling nearer.

Everett glanced recklessly behind himself, then back. "Jenny?"

Her pulse battered at her temples. "I can't."

"At the mall." He was pure steel. "Eleven o'clock."

She looked at the muscle knotted in his jaw. With a supreme exertion of self-control she set her mouth in a congealed smile.

"Have a pleasant chat, you two," she said, and shakily lifted her glasses from his hand without touching his fingers. "I won't be long."

There was nothing subtle about Mildred's consternation as she bustled about the kitchen. She clattered cups into saucers, slammed the top of the sugar bowl, and spilled cream on the surface of the counter. Presently, bracing the heels of slender hands that had worked hard for years, she leaned her weight upon them. Her head, elegant and graying, bowed.

Not knowing how to begin an explanation, or even if she should, Jenny mopped up the spilled cream without saying anything.

"I wasn't aware that Everett was back in town," Mildred said.

"He just got back today."

"It didn't take him long to find you, did it?"

"Oh, Mother."

"Don't 'Oh, Mother' me, Jenny. I stood by and watched your heart break over that boy once. You can't ask me to do it again. I couldn't stand it."

To keep her mother from seeing the battle raging inside her, Jenny busied herself with the silver. She inspected a spoon that was perfectly clean and rubbed furiously with a dish towel.

"Heartbreak?" she said brittlely. "Your conclusion's a little drastic, isn't it? Everett's in town on business. We happened to bump into each other, that's all."

Mildred made a clicking sound of disagreement. "You never could resist that boy."

"He's not a boy any longer, Mother. And that was a long time ago."

"I know it's a cliché to say I'm only thinking of your happiness, but I truly am. Your life is going along so well now, Jenny. I thought you and Ray were splendid together at dinner."

"Mother—"

"You deserve some happiness, Jenny. You're a young woman, and you work like a man. How do you think I feel, watching you drag yourself to bed at night, so burdened you're only half alive? I want you to have some of the good things before you're too old, like me."

Slipping beside her mother, placing an arm about a

waist that even now, at fifty-five, had not inordinately thickened, Jenny hugged Mildred.

"You're making too much of it. Everett's looking up a few old friends while he's in town. He's just been through a rather painful divorce, and I gather he—"

Mildred stepped back in horror. "A divorce! Oh, Jenny."

Jenny laughed a miserable, disheartened laugh. "Please don't say 'Like father, like son.'"

"But he will be, Jenny. The Black women are doomed to heartache."

"My goodness, you'd think the man had walked into my life and asked me to marry him! If it's any consolation, marriage is the furthest thing from Everett's mind. It's anathema to him, if you'd really like the truth. I've never seen anyone so bitter."

Having no idea if her answer had solved anything, Jenny ducked her head and started for the living room with the coffee. The telephone purred. Turning back, she paused.

Mildred answered, listened for a moment, then met her daughter's gaze with a combination of frustration and relief.

"It's for Everett," she said, obviously hoping the man was being called away.

"He told his service where he'd be. I'll get him."

Everett used the phone in the kitchen. It turned out to be one of those suspended times when everyone pretended not to overhear and couldn't help knowing everything. Ray, having been deserted in the living room, ambled haplessly in. Jeffrey poked his head in the door and got a glass of water he didn't want. And Stephen, choosing this moment to show his mother an advertisement for a home-built airplane that he thought was the answer to all their problems, stood beside Everett and flagrantly eavesdropped.

"How long ago?" Everett inquired into the receiver. One long-fingered brown hand rested absently upon Stephen's shoulder—an oddly paternal stance for a man with no children, it occurred to Jenny.

Everett's body abruptly stiffened. He caught the rung of a nearby chair with his heel and scooted it nearer, bracing his foot. Balancing a pad from his jacket upon one knee, he hurriedly began jotting down notes. The skirt of his jacket was pulled casually aside to reveal tightly pulled trousers and trimly muscled hips.

Jenny stood fascinated with an Everett Black she'd never seen before. He cut an expert, authoritative figure, his rapid-fire questions coming curtly and competently, his hands controlled and efficient. Realizing that she must look star-struck, she snatched her eyes away, then furtively looked at Ray to see if he'd caught her staring.

"Anyone killed?"

The silence grew deadly.

"Anyone hurt?" After a minute: "This really isn't my baby now, you know."

Ray's accusing frown met Jenny's. She wasn't certain if Ray envied Everett or not. She was certain he was piqued because she hadn't made an issue of their forthcoming engagement. She thought he was about to step near her.

Moving quickly, she proceeded to scrub the tabletop with the dish towel she still held. She heard every breath Everett drew.

"All right. Somebody has to. Get in a cleanup crew," he ordered in clipped tones. "Call the medical research councils involved and notify the prime minister of England. And the University of Cologne in West Germany too. Immediately. I'll scrape up everyone I can from the States and catch the next flight out. Hey, what about the equipment?"

There was a long pause. Then a soft "Damn." Another pause. "Okay, okay. I'll call the home office and see if I can get my man on loan from Bell Laboratories for the equipment."

Almost comically Everett found them all staring at him when he hung up. Their expressions, from friendly to resentful and all shocked, demanded an explanation.

He lifted one shoulder. "One of my projects," he said succinctly. "In Spain. Some terrorists blew up a dam in the north and caused a river to flood."

"Was the damage bad?"

"Disastrous."

"Tough luck," Ray remarked with a tactless look of sympathy.

Giving an impressed whistle, Stephen said, "Far out."

"But no one was hurt, you said." Jenny had stepped closer. Her concern was much more marked than she realized.

Everett talked as he scribbled on his note pad. "We've got about two million dollars' worth of ruined buildings on our hands. And almost total loss of sensitive equipment. The complex'll have to be gutted and salvaged, of course. As much as possible." Looking up, he heaved a sigh.

"I'm sorry," Jenny said, meaning it.

"Well, it can't be helped, I suppose."

"What a terrible waste," Mildred consoled before it dawned on her she was talking to the man she claimed to resent.

Absently scratching his jaw, Everett smiled at Mildred's lapse of prickliness.

"That's the word for it, Mrs. Stephenson. Waste.

Well, I guess I'd better get started putting a few technicians together. Repairing a wreckage is ten times worse than starting from scratch. You don't know anyone real good at patch jobs, do you?"

His question was a rhetorical one, not meant to be answered. Already he was replacing the telephone in its niche and moving toward the front of the house to leave.

Tagging behind Everett, partly because the new acquaintance was a man to admire and partly because his nine years tended to take random remarks at face value, Stephen said, "Mom is. When the Lancaster Hotel burned, she fixed it up all by herself. It's like brand new."

Jenny gave her youngest a visual warning to stop exaggerating. "I did have a little help, Stephen. Let's not get carried away."

"Of course," Everett mouthed slowly, as if his mind were racing through one calculation after another. "You're an interior designer. You're perfect for the job."

Jenny found herself as caught up as the rest. "What?"

"Normally Ruth would come in and help me, but . . ." Everett stopped thinking out loud as he realized he was skirting dangerous terrain.

"Who's Ruth?" demanded Mildred.

"Ahh . . . a member of the board who used to design the insides of the plant units themselves." Everett hurried on. "I'll pay you whatever price you say for two weeks' work, Jenny. But I can't give you any notice. I need it good, and I need it fast. Trouble-shooting, on the spot."

"You'd be great, Mom," encouraged the usually taciturn Jeffrey.

"Immediately?"

"Couldn't you get away?" Everett urged. "Don't you have any time coming where you are? I'll tell you, Jenny, I expect to find a nightmare on my hands over there. Skill from the States is almost impossible to find at a moment's notice. A half-dozen countries have invested in this, and they'll be on my back for repairs like hungry creditors."

Maternal panic edged Mildred's voice. "You can't take off from work just like that," she warned Jenny. "What would Pamela Chase do?"

"It's not the taking off, Mother. I could get the time. It's just that—"

"I'll make it well worth your employer's time to lend you to me, Jenny."

Ray plunged into the conversation like a pugilist expecting a knockout, fists up, head protected. "This is highly irregular, Jenny. Besides, it sounds dangerous. Terrorists? Those countries over there are so uncivilized."

Everett stifled a cough of protest. "For the most part the terrorists hide out in France. Don't get the idea that it's one big powder keg. It's usually very quiet. That's why we put our complex in this particular place."

"Doesn't sound quiet to me," grumbled Ray.

"You can't leave the boys," Mildred added with hard insistence. "Jeffrey's difficulty at school—" Her mouth clamped shut.

Instinctively knowing when a situation favored his own reluctance to have Ray for a father, Jeffrey popped out with, "Yes, she can. Stevie and I'll be fine, Grandma. Honest, Mom, we can do everything ourselves. School will be okay. I promise."

Ray and Mildred said at precisely the same moment, "But, Jenny—"

Nothing bowed Jenny's back more quickly than being told she couldn't do something.

"Look, everyone!" she cried, holding out both hands as if she would physically shove them away. "If I want to go to Spain and work for a couple of weeks, what's the harm in that? I work hard and rarely ask for anything. It's not going to hurt any of you if I take this assignment."

"It's okay with me if you go," Stephen pleasantly defended himself.

"But, Jenny—" Ray and Mildred said again.

Everett toyed with a poignant smile. This, except for Ray's unwanted opinion, was the type of bustling family caring he and Ruth had never shared. It hadn't even been in his own family.

"Say," he glanced about with unusual awkwardness, "you don't have a telephone book of Atlanta, do you?"

Jenny snapped up the excuse to escape her family for a few minutes. She stepped through the door toward the living room. "In here."

Once a wall separated them from the members of the family and Ray, Jenny experienced her earlier self-consciousness. She hurried toward a low table near the front windows. The prospects of being near Everett for two weeks had unleashed a flood of mixed feelings, the most volatile of which was her inability to resist him. Her mother was right: She'd never been able to. Was she insane to even be considering this?

From the periphery of her vision she could see Everett's legs positioned beside her right shoulder as she stooped for the book. His voice was a quiet murmur above her head. She didn't move. Surely he must hear the thunder of her heart beating.

"I want very much for you to come with me, Jenny," he said. "Please do."

"Why?" Remaining balanced on the balls of her feet, she placed the directory in her lap. She dug her fingers into the carpet to steady herself. "Why should I come with you?"

"Why not?"

"Ray Gerard, my mother, Stephen, Jeffrey."

"Jeffrey is fine. We understand each other. I need to talk to you about him, Jenny."

Amazed that he would say such a thing, Jenny came to her feet. Automatically Everett reached to help her. She disdained his help with a twist of her shoulder.

"Jeffrey's not your concern," she said curtly. "I see what you're doing, Everett, but it won't work. You can't get to me through my son."

Catching a sharp breath of anger, Everett flicked his gaze out at the room, then drilled it into her. "That's the most unfair thing I've ever heard you say. Jeffrey is an exceptionally bright boy. My guess is that he should be in a special school for the gifted."

Her laughter rippled bitterly. "Spoken like a wealthy man."

He drew down his mouth. "What has wealth got to do with it? You're about to marry a very wealthy man."

"Yes, I suppose I am."

"Oh, hell, Jenny. You don't love that man. Your mother does."

The tension sparkled through the room like a dozen floodlights coming on at once, blinding them.

"And that"—she hotly aimed her finger at the tip of his nose—"is the most unfair thing I've ever heard you say. Everett, why did you come here tonight?"

Wanting to break the tension before it worsened, Everett grabbed her offending finger. He forced her hand still, though she pulled back with surprising strength. Turning it over, baring its palm, he bent over it. With a fingertip he traced a path over the smooth surface.

He grinned up at her. "Do you know what it says here?"

Jenny found it difficult to sustain her exasperated pique in the face of such facetiousness. "No," she sighed, "and neither do you."

"Oh, yes, my darling. I know all, tell all." He pretended to ponder. "It says here . . . hm, that you're about to take a trip. A long trip, I see. And you wish that you'd gotten better grades in high school Spanish."

She made a protesting sound.

"Wait a minute, wait a minute," he said as she attempted again to retrieve her hand. "What's this? Ah, yes, the universal cure for all ills: *m-o-n-e-y*. I see you coming into a bit of money while abroad. Enough that you could get Jeffrey enrolled in a new school."

His brows lifted with shrewd solemnity. "I can do that, you know. For two weeks of your expertise I can pay you more than you'd earn in months where you are. It doesn't take an expert to see what you have in that son of yours, Jenny. He has special needs. You know that already."

Know it? She'd struggled with it for years. The temptation to trust him was strong: Adam tempting Eve with the apple.

"You see a lot in that hand, I think," she said breathlessly.

"There's more."

Everett, lips twitching impudently, bent over her hand once again, standing much nearer than was necessary this time. Only inches were separating them, and then there was his intoxicating, elusive scent.

The room was insufferably warm! Jenny's breath caught midway in her throat and refused to go any further.

"Here," he said, and traced a line. "A man. A dashing, handsome man. This handsome man—highly desirable by the looks of this, with a lot of fine, admirable qualities . . . No, no, be still. This man realizes you're still upset because of a certain kiss. He apologizes to you on bended knee. He promises that if you'll come with him, he'll be a paragon of virtue, impeccable in his conduct. He'll do nothing, say nothing, think nothing, that even smacks of impropriety."

Their eyes met over the touching hands, his teasing, hers struggling vainly to remain aloof. A sudden vacuum formed, a space where ignoring it was impossible and bearing it was unavoidable.

His teasing abruptly ceased. The telephone book slipped to the floor with a startling rustle of pages. Not flinching, he studied her shrinking expression—the way her lips parted, then compressed with dismay, the pinkness of her cheeks, the agitated rise and fall of her breasts beneath the sweater.

Jenny felt her own wonder softening the muscles beside her mouth. She took back her hand. Without consciously realizing it, she pressed it to the hollow of her throat and grew aware of a more internal response, one that had been hibernating for eight long years.

"What d'you say, Jen?" he urged huskily. "You know you'd like to go. It would help you and it'd help me. Is it a deal?"

"Everett Black"—she let her eyes close—"you are a persistent man. If I were to consider—" Her eyes flew wide. "—mind you, I said *consider*—working with you for two weeks, I'd want to be completely honest with you up front."

"Is this going to be one of those lectures for my own good?"

Her gaze narrowed. "Of course not. But we do have a history, Everett."

"Everyone's got a history."

"I'm not sure people ever get over one like ours."

What she should have said was that she hadn't gotten over it. He, obviously, suffered no such hang-ups other than a passing respect for it.

She plunged on. "I wouldn't want you to hope . . . How do I say this without embarrassing us both? It could never be like it was before. I have my boys to think of now, and a . . . oh dear, this is coming out all wrong." She felt him frowning at her. Without looking, she quickly added, "A relationship would be—"

"I hate the way people use that word."

"I don't know how else to put it. You know from what happened this afternoon that really painful things could occur between us. I don't need that. What I do need is money for Jeffrey." She grabbed a breath after such a raw exposure of her very soul. "That's the best I can do. Take it or leave it."

Everett wiped a hand across the back of his neck. There was nothing sophisticated about the way he reacted to her ultimatum. His whole body was rigid. "That's pretty honest, lady. It's also a bit unflattering to my morals."

"I didn't mean it to be. Oh, dammit, Everett, I'm twenty-eight years old. I can come to Spain. I can do a good job for you. But it wouldn't be an interlude. I have my life to come back to, the nitty-gritty realities."

"Ray."

"Jeffrey needs a father."

"The man's a banker, not a father!"

"He's the only one around who's asking! You don't have the right to an opinion in this!"

The muscles beside Everett's mouth leaped into thin, white ridges, but he didn't argue with her reasoning. It was true. What could he say? He gave her a tiny mock salute and took a step backward as if he'd been politely dismissed.

"Well, heck, ma'am," he said in a sultry Georgian

drawl, "now that everything's out in the open, I guess I'll just mosey back to the old hotel and get the flight schedule worked out."

Despite the fact that she'd done the honorable thing and placed her cards—face up—on the table, Jenny felt terrible. She groped at an excuse to change the subject.

"You said you had something to tell me," she blurted.

Taking a deep breath, knowing he could never tell her about the house now, Everett accepted the bitterness from her scars. He took it upon himself like a coat that was too big but must be worn because it's the only thing around.

"I guess it wasn't that important," he said.

"Oh, Everett, don't be like that."

"Like what?"

She had to press her foot to keep from stamping it. Sighing, she said, "You didn't use the telephone book."

His head came up. "What telephone book?"

"Ohh!"

Everett looked at the door to the kitchen as if it were a sudden enemy. When he turned back he spoke quickly, urgently. "I swear to God, Jenny, I never meant to hurt you all those years ago. I'd take it all back if I could." His hand closed over hers. "Then . . . well, we were kids. Kids do crazy things. But I'm sorry. From the bottom of my heart."

In a gesture of sheer recklessness, Everett clasped her by the shoulders as she was turning away.

Jenny had never thought she would hear those words. She let him turn her back as easily as a swath of fine silk.

"Mother?" Jeffrey poked his head in the door, the lower half of his body remaining in the dining room.

Everett jerked his hands off Jenny as if he'd been caught stealing.

Startled, Jenny stepped away as her head came round. "What is it?" she replied in a strange faraway voice.

"Is it all right for Grandma to take us to the arcade while you pack?" The boy grinned at Everett. "I need to work on my score."

"That arcade gets too many of my quarters, Jeffrey Howard." Jenny felt the rush of relief of fretting over her children. Thank God for children! "And I haven't decided to go to Spain yet."

Everett fished in his pocket and drew out a handful of loose change. "Yes, she has. The final details were just worked out. Here now, Jeff." He counted out several quarters into the youngster's hand. "What your mother doesn't understand is that there are some necessities in a man's life that can't be avoided."

When Jeffrey smiled he looked like a beautiful angel. "Hey, thanks. Are you coming back to town soon?"

Everett walked with Jeffrey back through the door. Pausing, his frame reaching nearly to the top of the opening, he considered the house he'd just bought for this boy's mother.

"I expect I will, Jeffrey. I expect I will." He motioned to Jenny. "Are you coming to pack now?"

The messages that telegraphed from one to the other needed no more words. Everett had no misconceptions about where he stood with her, but he wanted her to come more than he'd wanted anything for a long time. And Jenny, knowing Everett would never feel about her the way she felt about him, accepted the inevitable truth. She could, and would, keep things on a level professional keel. They could help each other in a realistic way. What could be the harm? And the future with Ray? She would work that out when she returned from Spain.

Chapter Four

Spain, it was said, was shaped like the hide of a bull. The neck pointed toward Africa in the south, and the rear end was formed by the Pyrenees mountains and the Bay of Biscay in the north. That was romantically fitting, Jenny thought: Spain, the mother of dashing matadors and brilliant flamenco dancers and soldiers of fortune like Balboa and Cortez. Others pictured Spain as a lady of mystery dressed in jet-black velvet, tempting men to seduce her with the glory of their Western inventions—also a romantic depiction.

Romance aside, before their plane touched down in Barcelona—by way of Madrid—Jenny knew she'd made one of the worst miscalculations of her life.

In the terminal she gazed wearily at a teeming potpourri of people. Even though the two million annual tourists hadn't yet swarmed over Spain's beaches, many of the faces she saw now were not Basque. And many of the languages she heard were not Castilian or the Catalan spoken in Barcelona. They had one thing in common: Most of the travelers looked as tired as she was. It wasn't the jet lag that plagued her, though.

She kept close to Everett's side. "I had no idea Barcelona was so . . ."

"European?"

"It's almost like trying to get around in New York City or London."

He eyed her with amused suspicion. "I didn't know you'd been to London."

"I haven't. But I'm sure this is the way it is."

He laughed at the simplicity of her logic.

She paused a moment to shuffle her leather tote bag higher on her shoulder.

Everett, walking past, realized she wasn't following. He stopped and shifted his weight with the flex of a hip, his garment bag slung over his back. "What's the matter, Jenny?" he called back. "Where's your spirit of high adventure?"

It never came at a good time. She stared at the rugged, masculine beauty of him standing there like some vagabond pirate and knew that her desire for this man was as impelling as it had ever been. The truth was—and she was ready to admit it after battling it ever since they had left Atlanta—all her talk of propriety had been a self-deceptive veneer. And *that* was what coiled inside her like a dangerous, overwound spring.

She masked her attraction to him with a counterfeit levity. "Don't stand there looking like a zany Marco Polo. It doesn't impress me. And my spirit of adventure drowned somewhere in the Atlantic Ocean. I'm really bushed, Everett."

"Does that mean you don't want to disco at the Metamorfosis after dinner?" He braced a hand on his hip in an exaggerated disappointment. "I was so looking forward, Jen."

"You can disco on the top of Puerta de la Paz if you want to," referring to the city's 200-foot-high monument to Columbus. "I want only a peanut butter sandwich and a good bed."

They stepped through the doors to face the largest of the Mediterranean seaports. The weather, compared to the bitter cold they'd left behind, was surprisingly mild. Everett tossed her a glance over his shoulder—one of the many proper and sterile glances he'd given her since leaving the States.

"The bed I can promise you. The Hotel Gaudí is tasteful, spacious, and steam-heated. The peanut butter sandwich? You might have to settle for gazpacho and paella."

Jenny smirked at his irony.

He shrugged elegantly. "Cold soup and saffron rice with seafood. Barcelona's famous for its paella. Then to bed early. I promise. It may surprise you to know, darling, that despite my hardy virility I'm a bit weary myself."

"Am I allowed a bath first?"

"Only if you really need it." He grinned.

"Sadist."

Dressing for dinner, Jenny put on a coral silk blouse and fluffed her hair until wisps of ringlets framed her face. Nice, she thought. Not voluptuous, but nice. She buttoned a cardigan sweater and pulled on a corduroy blazer. The overall effect was too efficient; she looked like somebody's secretary. She pursed her mouth and stared at the top button of her blouse. Quickly, before she could change her mind, knowing exactly why she was doing it, she undid the top button and smoothed the bodice until it displayed the space between her breasts. The cleavage was subtle but there—a pale, shadowy temptation.

"Hello," Everett said, smiling as he waited good-naturedly outside her room.

He was enormously attractive in his red turtleneck sweater and houndstooth-check sport coat, cut to perfection. His gray slacks weren't pleated but fit smoothly over his stomach. The hems, brushing upon the tops of his shoes with a smart, casual look, said "I don't take myself seriously, but everyone else had better."

"Are you hungry?"

Perilously attuned to his reactions, Jenny made a graceful pirouette after she had shut the door. Nerves quivered in her stomach. She gave her head an eloquent, smiling toss.

"I'm starved. Am I dressed right, do you think?"

A nerve ticked at Everett's temple.

Searching for the wicked twinkle in his blue eyes, Jenny held her breath.

A heartbeat passed.

"You're fine," he said hesitantly as another of his bland smiles curved his lips. "Is your room all right? If it's not, let me know and I'll have something done about it. Or we can have you moved to another. They're quite nice about—"

Jenny's fragile coquetry disintegrated like gray smoke. "The room's perfect," she snapped with the frozen correctness she reserved for men like Alan Kendall.

She'd done it again—reached out to him, exposing herself in a dreadful, raw way. It was the last time, damn him! she swore fervently. The absolute last time!

Everett said nothing more. He strolled beside her across the lobby without so much as a casual brush of a shoulder against hers. He hailed a taxi and helped her inside with only the most chaste support beneath her elbow.

Well, did she have anyone to blame but herself? No one had made her lay down the rules. She'd come to this place knowing full well how sticky it could get. She couldn't be a whiner. Lifting trembling fingers to the front of her blouse, wishing wretchedly that she was alone in her room, she covertly rebuttoned the top button.

Throughout dinner her acting merited a critic's award. She smiled and complimented the excellence and ignored the bad. With her heart heavy, she forced herself to sparkle. A number of men's heads turned casually to watch her, catching her eye when they could while trying not to attract the attention of their companions. One man even covertly held her gaze in a blatant three-second seduction of his own behind his menu. Everett appeared infuriatingly oblivious.

In spite of their sleepy exhaustion and the steadily increasing tedium of their cordiality, dinner in Catalonia's chief city turned out to be quite pleasant. Everett's expertise with the language—once outlawed and now spoken with pride by Barcelona's nationals—was passable. He amused the waiter who, instead of being disdainful of the "riffraff," was used to the French, Britons, Germans, and Americans struggling with his native tongue. The waiter went out of his way to give excellent service. Everett's tip was handsome.

Leaning back on the seat of the taxi on the way back to the hotel, agreeably sated with a dessert of tea cakes and sangria, Jenny watched Everett as he reacquainted himself with the city. He leaned forward and braced his elbows on the seat to talk to the driver. When the driver learned they were traveling inland the next day, he began chattering about the now-dead President Franco.

"Franco died on November 20, 1975," he said in heavily accented English. "Nothing in this country has worked right since."

Everett smiled. "Give it time. Your democracy is very young."

"But I am not so young, señor," the driver came back. "What is this with terrorists blowing up reservoirs? No one is happy anymore."

Everett let the question go unanswered. He placed his arm along the back of Jenny's seat but didn't drop it upon her shoulder.

"Sleepy?"

"Mmm." She kept her face averted and pretended to observe the street. His constant, untouchable nearness was eroding her. She bit her lips, feeling the full weight of her failure in coming here.

"Anything you'd like to do before I take you back?" he asked. "We leave early in the morning, otherwise I'd take you to a cabaret. You should see at least one Gypsy dance in her tight *traje de lunares.*"

The taxi driver, eavesdropping shamelessly, bobbed his head in agreement.

Jenny finally yielded to the tugs of motherhood. "Would it be all right if I sacrificed the Gypsies for one call home?"

"Driver," called Everett. "Let us out here, please."

They walked the remaining blocks to the hotel. At the first sight of a public telephone they stopped. While Jenny seated herself on a bench and wondered how to go about dealing with the operator, Everett positioned himself in the doorway.

"You could do this better at the hotel," he suggested.

She frowned at the instructions on the telephone. "I want to do it here."

Wanly attempting humor, she added, "This way I

can pretend I'm a heroine in a James Bond spy thriller, in Europe on some incredibly dangerous mission."

"And you're calling the home office, 007?"

Momentarily distracted, her curly head craned about as a Saab zoomed past them on the boulevard. "Europeans look so terribly clandestine in the movies. Don't you love the sound of their foreign cars?"

He chuckled. "Over here they're not foreign, Jenny."

She wasn't listening; she was scowling at the telephone again. "Everett, I don't know how to do this."

He grinned as she squinted. Laughing, he said, "It isn't that you can't do it, dear, you can't *see* it. Where're your glasses?"

Squeezing himself behind her in the booth, he braced an arm beside her head to form a muscular trap with his body. His other hand, when he leaned over her shoulder to point, lightly grazed her jaw.

Jenny stilled with the abruptness of having heard an intruder on a dark night. What was he doing? The muscles spanning his trunk were pressing against her shoulder blades. She could feel the large curved bones as if some witch's wand had suddenly traced them with fire into her flesh. She should move away, she thought distractedly. She should behave as if the touching were an accident. But wasn't this what she'd wanted all evening?

Turning, she found her temple scored by his belt buckle. The smell of soap on his hands blended with the more acrid pungency of the leather of his belt. Something stirred inside her, something charged and frightening and alive.

She gripped the receiver numbly. "I didn't mean you had to—"

"Spain purposely designs these things like this," he

chuckled with soft irony. Then, as if he knew what she had just felt, he drew back the necessary inches so that he didn't touch her. "They're a closely knit people, the Spanish."

"I . . ." She swallowed with difficulty. "I can see that."

She let her eyes close as she waited for the operator. *Oh, Everett,* she wanted to say, *if it's my lifeblood you want, why don't you make a clean kill?* "Hello, Jeffrey, is that you? This is Mother. Can you hear me?"

Everett stared down at the top of Jenny's bent head and grappled with the frustration that had plagued him all through dinner and now. Why was he feeling left out, like some rejected kid? He'd been the one who'd made it clear he wanted nothing permanent with a woman. He should be glad she had put up the boundaries before they ever left the States. Yet, he wasn't. They depressed him. They made him resent a ten-year-old boy for being able to arouse that sweet, loving energy in her voice.

Her shoulder moved. His waist instantly tightened. Her touch sent a sudden ache stirring through him and made him want to bury his fingers into her curls and kiss the top of her head. But he only stood thinking of Martin Howard, a man he didn't even know. Was he . . . jealous of Martin? Did he wish, deep in his heart of hearts, that Jenny was calling home to check on their own children?

Fool! he called himself. He'd done the right thing in maintaining his hands-off stance on the flight over. It hadn't been easy. For long hours he'd sat beside her, longing to hold her. He'd borne the weight of her head when it, with unknowing intimacy, dropped to his shoulder as she dozed. It had put his arm to sleep. Yet, he'd sat treasuring the pain of it. He'd listened, in a half-state of arousal, to her small rustling sounds when she shifted in her seat. Even the way her fingers curled in her lap turned him on. Had Martin been a good lover? Jenny had always required time to reach fulfillment. Had Martin taken the care she needed? Or perhaps Jenny had needed the time only back then, only with him. Maybe it was his own clumsy inexperience. . . . Damn, he couldn't go on thinking like this!

At length, when Jenny slowly replaced the receiver, she dropped her forehead against the telephone. The nape of her neck unconsciously invited his kiss. He was so caught up in his private misery that his hands were reaching for her, his lips were lowering before he realized what he was doing.

He straightened like the spent string of a bow. For a fleeting moment he held his hands extended, then dropped them to his sides.

"Oh, God," she sighed with poignant homesickness. "My heart breaks for Jeffrey. He's so sensitive. So open to pain."

He tried to clear the raspiness from his voice. "He'll learn how to deal with it."

"I don't know if he will. I see him going through his whole life impatient with people, never tolerating them very well, being a permanent stranger no matter where he is."

There was no way he could remove that maternal suffering from her. He hurt for her, but he couldn't save her from it.

"Sometimes I awake in the night, panic-stricken about what will happen to my children. They love me. They think I can do everything. And I can't, Everett. There are times I think I can't help at all. It's . . ."

He trembled from the tremendous effect she was having over him. "Exhausting?" His voice cracked.

She twisted around to peer up at him, her eyebrows

to the center. "Is that awful? For a mother to say her children's love exhausts her?"

"All love is exhausting."

He spoke with such utter honesty that she believed him completely.

As they walked the rest of the way to the hotel, Jenny cast curious, sidelong glances at Everett, wondering at his even deeper withdrawal. Once he caught her studying him. He smiled bleakly. Then he jerked his gaze straight ahead.

An abnormal intensity gripped them both as they waited for the light to change. Neither moved a muscle but simply stood, excruciatingly aware of their previously agreed-upon obligations to avoid the other.

"Sorry," she said when her hand swung into his.

Everett didn't reply. He grasped her hand, which shocked her. She didn't dare look at him as they reached the other side. He didn't release her hand as she thought he would, but laced his fingers through hers and held it firmly at his side. His palm, warm and dry, reminded her of the first time he'd held her hand at the movies. He'd placed his hand on his own knee next to hers and inched toward it with a pretense that was ridiculous, for neither of them could think of anything else.

Oh, Lord, why hadn't he wanted to marry her?

"Did you love her very much?" she asked.

The question was out before Jenny could stop it. She had thought about it ever since she had heard Ruth mentioned by name, but had never dreamed she would actually ask it.

Everett was oblivious to the wave of people that parted and passed around them as if they were an island. "I don't know. Did you love Martin?"

"Yes."

She wanted to add that it was a different love than what she'd once felt for him. She wanted to say it was a settled, logical love that she and Martin grew into because he was the father of her children. If she had dared, she would have said, *I respected and loved Martin. I worshiped you.*

The entrance of the hotel seemed to appear out of the blue. Neither of them felt the increasing chill. They didn't notice that people were waiting behind them to get through the doors.

Pulling her hand free, Jenny put it, tingling, into her coat pocket as they crossed the lobby. She made a fist. Deep inside her the low ache was settling, and she knew why. He mustn't suspect.

"How did you meet Ruth?" He didn't want to talk about his ex-wife, she knew, but talking about Ruth was better than the destruction of the silence.

"At a dinner for a state senator. Her family was high on the social structure, and I was a fledgling business-man trying to get ahead. You know—the ambition to be more than my parents were."

"I guess I don't. Martin had nothing and I had nothing. We lived in a tiny apartment over a depart-ment store for a year."

He shook his head. "It was a mistake from the beginning. As I look back I think . . . I don't know what I thought. I liked her father more than I did Ruth, I guess. Elston was good to his wife, and I admired that. I still like him. He taught me a lot."

"But not enough?"

Everett peered down at her in puzzlement. "What d'you mean?"

Jenny pushed the elevator button, then faced him before the doors could swish open.

"He didn't teach you how to be happy, Everett. He

may have taught you how to succeed, but he didn't teach you to be happy."

"Happiness isn't an acquired skill, my dear."

The elevator door thrust them into a small, incubated world that prohibited private talk. Not until they had gotten out and were standing outside her door, Jenny fishing the key from her purse, did they pick up the thread that dangled between them. Jenny faced him with a directness she wouldn't have guessed she was capable of.

"What would it take to make you happy, Everett?" she asked as she held the key poised over the lock. "I really want to know."

At first she thought he was going to touch her. He shifted his weight as if he was preparing to take her in his arms. She saw something pass over his eyes: a mask? a warning?

She leaned backward, away from him, her key extended like a tiny weapon.

The lines of tension at Everett's eyes relaxed momentarily as a quick, sad smile curved up the edges of his mouth. He lifted the key from her fingers and inserted it into the lock. It tumbled with a click and he pushed it open. Opening her palm, he placed the key into it and closed her fingers securely about it.

"You would make me happy," he said thickly, and turned abruptly on his heel.

He didn't look back as she watched him walk away.

Jenny knew, as she entered her room and leaned back against the door, that she should never have asked him such a question. *You would make me happy*. What did it matter? She had let it happen, knowing full well that it was possible. She had fallen head over heels in love with Everett Black again.

* * *

The next day their rented car dutifully snarled its way through the traffic threading inland from the Spanish coast. The congestion was merciless. The explosion at the reservoir further north had sent twenty-nine cubic miles of renegade water over the countryside. Thirty thousand people were homeless, and damages were estimated at $193 million. Some of the railroads and highways were underwater. Detours and waits beside the road seemed the order of the day. And that under the direction of a weary and badly organized police force.

Everett's temper smoldered until his silences said more than his occasional muttered curses. And Jenny's counterfeit serenity seriously began to erode.

"As soon as I reach the next town," he said, consulting the map Jenny had spread on the seat, "I'm going to try to get a helicopter. This is ridiculous."

"Couldn't we have flown to the site of the plant?"

"Air travel isn't as extensive as in other places. Since the tourists stay mainly on the beaches, travel to the small towns is mostly by car or train."

His attempts to charter a helicopter were as futile as driving to the site. Every unit, he was informed, was in the air on emergency details. And telephone connections to the laboratory were almost as impossible as getting a helicopter; only one line was intact. Finally, after an hour's delay, he did speak with someone at the disaster site and told him he was trying to make it in.

"We're not the only ones having trouble," he reported as he returned to the car where Jenny waited, tired. He stood, one foot braced on the car, one foot on the ground, and squinted out at the traffic. "Our people trying to get over the French border are having it just as tough."

Jenny dragged her eyes from the way his trousers

tightened to outline his wallet in his hip pocket, the way his fingers spread over the bend of his knee. She consulted her wristwatch.

"It's been eight hours," she said. "And we're still twenty-five miles from the complex."

Everett clapped the muscles in the back of his neck and heaved a sigh. The stress was taking its toll.

"Perhaps if you had something to eat," she carefully suggested. They'd not eaten since breakfast in Barcelona.

Crawling in beside her, he slammed the door shut. He draped his arm behind her seat. Jenny was positive he didn't realize that he was smoothing the corduroy nap at the back of her jacket.

"This is a damned way to see Spain, isn't it?"

"I didn't come for a pleasure trip, Everett," she said, letting her eyes run over his darkening stubble of beard. "I came to help."

"Then would you mind rubbing hard, right there?"

Turning, he presented his back and drew a line over the muscles branching from his neck into his shoulders.

In her present state of mind he couldn't have asked a more difficult thing of her. She'd been battling her fantasies of him all day. Touching him was a cruelty.

Catching her lip between her teeth, endeavoring to hide the flush creeping up from her waist, Jenny laid her purse aside. She gripped the tops of his shoulders and kneaded with a firm, steady motion that soon had Everett growling with relief.

"Up a little," he rumbled, letting his head drop to his chest and giving a moan of pleasure when she found the right spot.

Jenny's eyes slid out of focus. How brutal her memories were: his bare back, broad and flexing with muscles as she smoothed suntan lotion on it at the lake, his chest that was matted sparsely with night-dark curls, the way he rolled over and threw a leg across her waist and braced himself on his hands beside her shoulders, smiling down. Dear God, was he so insensitive that he couldn't feel how torturous this was for her?

Beneath her hands the tension seeped from Everett like a mist. He shifted his weight and let his shoulders slump backward against her. The crown of his head, half turning, brushed against the curve of her chin, almost as if his cheek were searching for the cushion of her bosom. Before she could move away from him her nipples tightened with an aching readiness. She knew he had to feel them.

"There!" she exclaimed with harrowed briskness. She gave him a slap on the shoulder. "Good as new."

Swiveling, dragging her leg free, facing her window in a bundle of nerves, she pressed her nose out of shape against the glass. *Ask me what's wrong,* she prayed silently. *Ask me and I'll tell you the truth.*

For some minutes Everett said nothing. He read her anguish exactly, for he was feeling the same thing. He felt it battering against him like hailstones and didn't dare look anywhere except at his hands shaking upon the steering wheel. Presently he could control his voice enough to speak.

"I'll keep working on the chopper," he said gruffly. "Meanwhile let's eat and at least get a place to sleep."

"That's a good idea." She didn't care what he did.

"Maybe something will change by morning."

"Maybe the terrorists will blow up a dam farther south and all the water will drain off."

Everett chuckled lamely. "I'm afraid it doesn't work that way, darling."

Her eyes blazed as she twisted her head around. "Don't call me that!"

He cocked his head. "What?"

"*That.*"

"Darling? Well, hell, Jenny . . ."

Oh, God, she thought desperately, now he would figure everything out. Or perhaps he wouldn't. Perhaps he was so immersed in his own selfishness that he would be blind to her love.

Lifting her hand to a curl, she strategically kept it between Everett and herself. She gathered the courage to address the impossible tension between them. "I don't believe I realized until now," she said with strained difficulty, "how naive I've been all my life."

Since she couldn't see him, she listened for a change in his breathing—a movement, anything. Everett was perfectly still.

"I've been reacting badly throughout this whole trip, Everett. I . . . I keep forgetting I'm an adult, not that flitter-brained girl underneath that silly willow tree. I don't really have an excuse. I'm sorry."

He cleared his throat and let his hand rest on the car keys in the switch. Once he started to turn the engine over, then he waited.

She lowered her hand. "I've made a bad mistake, Everett."

"Are you saying you want to go back home?"

"I should."

Everett's hand grasped the key in the ignition as if it were a foe. He twisted and the engine blazed to life. He jammed the gearshift in place, hesitated, then slammed into Park again. He jerked off the ignition.

The kiss happened before either of them was consciously prepared for it. His lips were hardly sensual but ravenous and driving to reassure himself that she was there. He filled her quickly with his taste. It was his hands that sent Jenny's heart plunging into her feet—the release of their crushing hold of her head, their hesitance upon her shoulders, their move to her breasts, their brief, flitting caress as he curved them about her. As if stung, then, his breath tore. He snatched his hands away and held them slightly extended as if he weren't sure if they were his.

Jenny sat stunned, breathing hard, unable to cope with her own distorted impulses, much less Everett's.

"I . . ." Everett straightened himself in his seat and fit his feet against the floorboard. His fingers tightened and relaxed about the steering wheel, tightened and relaxed. Bouncing one palm off the rim, he presently sighed and said, "I guess we'd better get something to eat."

Jenny still hadn't moved. What could she do? What could she say? What could either of them say, when they both realized this couldn't go on much longer.

Their dinner at Talencia's one overcrowded cafe, though it was early for dining, was more uncomfortable than the hours it had taken to get there. Jenny didn't taste a bite she put in her mouth. She was deliriously glad to see the end of it.

"I'm sorry, señor."

The Basque matron apologized from the desk of a small, unpromising hotel squeezed between the market and a three-story apartment building. The sound of arguing, laughter, and busy talking drifted from the uneven streets outside. The sun, far past its zenith, shone with difficulty through the film on the windows. Peasant women drifted past on the street, their wide black skirts complementing their drab head coverings. Donkeys dominated the streets as much as the automobiles and caused horns to blare and men's voices to rise and arms to wave.

"There are no single rooms available," the woman was saying. "It's the flooding. Once the highway opens up . . ."

She threw her hand toward the ceiling in an impetuous gesture meaning everyone was expected to make sacrifices in such an emergency.

"What did she say?" Jenny lifted worried eyes to Everett.

"There aren't any single rooms."

"No single rooms available?" Jenny repeated the words dumbly.

Understanding, the woman made a circle with her thumb and forefinger and shook her head with its gleaming black hair piled high. Her ivory-crusted combs winked. Diamonds? wondered Jenny. In Talencia? It was doubtful.

"Our gentlemen guests are bunking together in some of the rooms and the ladies are doubling, no less than two to a room. We have two double rooms left. Or I can give you a roommate."

Jenny figured out the exchange in a daze. "Perhaps another hotel?" she suggested behind her hand, her voice low. "I don't want to room with some strange woman."

Everett asked about another hotel.

Looking over their shoulders at other waiting customers, the matron grew brusque. She shook her head again. "Some of the families are taking an overnight boarder. But there are no rooms, señora. As these people will tell you."

Jenny met the woman's eyes as if she would like to throw the soiled hotel register at her.

The matron shrugged. "I'm sorry," she said with sincere generosity. A wisp of humor suddenly appeared in her eye. "But for such a handsome man, señora?" She patted her bulge below her waist to indicate her approval of Everett's trim waist and flat stomach. "Perhaps you could come to an . . . . agreement for an emergency."

Behind them irritable adults shuffled their feet. Weary children, several of whom were Americans, complained of having to go to the bathroom and of weariness and hunger. Jenny knew they would be glad to get a double room under any circumstances.

"This has to be the most insane thing," she mumbled.

Everett's smile teased one corner of his mouth. He held up his palms in infuriating innocence. "Don't look at me, dar—I mean, Jenny. I didn't plan it."

"It wouldn't surprise me if you had."

"Will you be taking the room, señor?"

"We'll take it."

"Everett!"

He turned his shoulder as he fished out his wallet.

The woman, already motioning the next family forward, filled out her form and accepted the deposit before the hesitant American could object.

"I, for one, am bone tired," Everett said meaningfully, keeping his head averted so no one could hear but her. "Having designs upon your body is the furthest thing from my mind. We're taking the room."

She compressed her lips tightly together.

Her persistent uncooperation under these circumstances annoyed Everett. "Do you have any better suggestions?"

Jenny thought she could suggest driving back to Barcelona and taking the same flight out that they had come in on. But even that wouldn't solve the problem of resting when they were too tired to go another step.

"My suggestion isn't printable, Everett, much less speakable."

Wincing, he signed his name across the form with a flourish.

"Have a pleasant stay with us, señor," the woman

called after him as Everett looked for a man to help with the luggage. He nodded his thank you and thought it was probably better for his masculine image that the Basque woman had no idea of the problems he would undoubtedly face this night.

The room was so tiny, the bed nearly covered the entirety of the floor space. A portable closet occupied one corner and a stuffed chair the other. The room beside the single window was, she hoped, the bathroom. The dressing table was a box draped with a cloth, and the decoration consisted of one framed print above the bed—a Michelangelo, oddly enough—and a hand-painted vase with some plastic daffodils in it.

Yet, everything was clean, even if it was Spartan. Walking to the closet, she opened it up. An extra pillow and blanket lay blessedly in the bottom. That might prove to be a solution to at least one of their problems.

As Everett and the man brought up their luggage, she clasped her hands behind her back and stared out of the second-story window. The rice plantations stretched out like marshes around the farms. The modest whitewashed walls caught the lazy afternoon sun. Far in the distance a silvery-pink lake blended into the sky. The boat of an eel fisherman cut a disdainful silhouette against the skyline as he poled his craft among the reeds. He appeared not to notice that his quiet town was jarred out of its serenity by strange cars sending dust to settle upon straw roofs and by bored, impatient travelers who were out and about to see what they could, since they were trapped in a town miles from their destination. Overhead, occasional helicopters rumbled across the sky on their way toward the flood site.

Everett walked into the room and shut the door. He inspected the cramped quarters as if they were the last thing his frayed temper could be asked to bear. He brushed his hands of dust, then idly scratched his jaw.

"Well, Jenny girl, if you plan on bathing this evening, I suggest you don't wait too long. I have my doubts about the water supply once these increased demands are made upon it."

That was exactly what she wanted to do. Carefully opening her suitcase upon the bed, she removed some clean underthings and a fresh sweater. Not only did she herself have doubts about the hot water, but the radiator crouching near the wall looked suspiciously temperamental.

When she emerged, dressed but damp, having braved lukewarm water and a hurried scrubbing, Jenny moved to stand before the mirror. A towel was draped softly about her neck. Lifting it with both hands, she began blotting her clean, dripping curls. In the reflection she caught Everett sitting cross-legged in the center of the bed.

He was shirtless and tousled, his elbows resting on his knees. A dark red stain was inching slowly up the muscles of his neck. Jenny felt as if she'd been captured by time-lapse photography as she followed the path of his stare.

When she glanced back at herself—her lifted arms, her breasts thrust into prominence, her sweater pulled above the waist of her slacks to reveal a very pale, very glaringly bare abdomen—the words they'd said in the car seemed like a presentiment. To jerk down the sweater would be to call attention to their awareness. To stand there was to invite disaster. She held her breath.

Caught unexpectedly with no barriers to protect him, Everett let his eyes flick hungrily from Jenny's mouth, over her breasts, down the clinging fit of her slacks, over her buttocks, to her bare feet and back up. A deep furrow slashed between his brows, and he took in a short, harsh breath and wet his lips. Then he threaded the fingers of his right hand through his hair and left it untidily rumpled.

She saw his desire—blatant, total. Even though she'd tried to arouse him to the point of . . . what? Flirtation? A pass? Some ego-satisfying declaration? She wasn't at all equipped for the passion that turned his eyes a dark, intense slate and made him look like a predator that could stalk her down until he slaked his lust with her.

She jerked down her arms. As unobtrusively as she could she pulled the sweater down about her hips. Without turning she heard his curse muttered under his breath. She kept her head down for fear of what he would say, but she glimpsed him cramming a stack of papers back into his briefcase. He threw the case into the corner and, without looking at her again, disappeared into the bathroom. He shut the door with a hard, sharp slam.

Neither bandied words when he reappeared fifteen minutes later.

"Put on a jacket."

"Why?"

"We're taking a drive into the mountains. I need to get out of this room."

Jenny, grabbing up her blazer, swiftly agreed. He didn't need to leave the room nearly as badly as she did.

They spent the next hour driving over the farmlands and high up into the hill country surrounding Talencia. Once they stopped and talked to a farmer and admired his rice crop. The wizened old man offered to take them out in his boat, but the sun was dipping lower and lower in the west. Everett said they wanted to see the old castle ruins before it got too dark.

The old man gazed up at the remnants of a castle on a hill overlooking the valley. He stroked the wisps of a beard. "The prince was a murderer, you know," he said, shaking his head. "Killed his three wives."

When Everett translated this, Jenny grimaced and hugged herself. Perhaps the prince thought he'd had his reasons. She started to ask how the prince met his own end, but decided to let the mystery go unsolved. That was part of the charm of this land; it oozed dark rumors and unspeakable secrets. Had lovers secretly gone up to the ruins as she and Everett were about to do? she wondered. Had the old prince caught his wives being held by forbidden lovers' arms?

"Hold my hand," Everett warned some minutes later as he helped her climb over the craggy stone pillars that spilled across the slope of the terrain. "All I need is for you to go back to your mother with a broken limb."

The castle had obviously consisted of three floors with a keep on one end. The keep was still intact, but the floors were hardly more than partial ledges jutting out of the remaining shell of walls. Part of a stairway lined one wall. A hill of stones and mortar lay beside another of the walls, which, if one climbed it, gave access to a sizable ledge that was the third floor. The best vantage of seeing the countryside would be gotten from the third floor.

Grasping her hand, Everett practically dragged her up to what had been the second story. From there they clawed their way to the third. Now they could gaze down the valley of springing gorges before it erupted out into the flatlands of the farmers. The view was breathtaking, a contrast of wildness and gentle pastoral serenity.

He sighed. "It's times like this when I look back over my life and I see very little besides a great collection of rubble."

Jenny stood behind his left shoulder, hugging herself from the wind. "Nature does that. It's like the night—strips everything bare of makeup."

Peering over his shoulder, he reproved her with an amused narrowing of his eyes. "Your short life requires a lot of makeup, does it?"

She smiled at his sleeve. "Mine needs a whole face lift."

She began picking her way through the collection of broken stones. Finding a place to sit where she could support her back, she bent, dusted it, and settled herself. She leaned her head back against a wall.

"Why do you think I'm so innocent, Everett?" she called to him. "Because I don't have a divorce in my repertoire of mistakes? Is divorce the only crime one can commit?"

The solitude was casting a tranquil spell. Joining her, Everett lowered himself and braced his back against the same stone. Beside his foot, in a collection of earth blown out of place by the wind, stood spires of grass dead from the winter. The blades were as unexpected as finding a fruit orchard on a Manhattan rooftop. He snapped off a twig and began systematically peeling it to pieces.

Jenny sat entranced with the beauty of his hands, wishing she dared take them in hers, kiss them, and tell him everything would be all right.

"It's the failure of divorce," he said presently. "It's just so . . . uncontrollable. Even when I juggle money that refuses to be adequate, as inflexible as that is, it's not as futile as seeing a marriage crumble in your hands. No matter how it turns out, you see yourself doing and saying things, and you know, deep down, that that was the reason it died."

He tossed the twig away and picked another. This one he clamped between his teeth and chewed on, deeply immersed in his memories.

"I used to look at my dad," he said, as if talking to himself, "and I told myself I'd never hurt a woman like he hurt my mother. I kept this mental list of his abuses and I swore to myself I'd never be guilty of them. Now I could run a checklist and they'd turn out to be the story of my life."

"That feeling isn't unique to divorce, Everett."

"I tell myself that." He smiled in self-mockery. "Every day I say, 'Buck up, Everett, old boy. You gave it one hell of a try.'"

"Didn't you?"

He brushed off the crust of his self-pity. The lines about his mouth softened. "Yes."

With a tiny ceremony he lifted her hand from her lap and placed their palms together. He studied the differences in their lengths for a moment, then spread her hand upon the shelf of his knee. Smoothing it, following the miniature valleys and peaks between her fingers, he sighed.

Jenny guessed it wasn't only his divorce that weighed upon him. The responsibilities of his work were even more grievous. Most men couldn't or wouldn't bear them. She didn't know how to comfort him and she wanted to badly. Her hand began shaking.

She gripped his knee, as if she were connecting with the bones beneath the flesh, the stone roots of his body.

Everett, pulling her eyes up to his with the sheer strength of his will, saw the sympathy on her face. He removed the twig from his mouth and tossed it away. He spat a sliver of grass.

She forced a fragile laugh. "You'd make a good mother, Everett. I think all of us have looked at other children and said, 'My child will never do that.' And guess what they invariably do."

The wind was whipping his hair about his forehead, heightening the sensual appeal of his moodiness. Unconsciously he smoothed it back, only to have it tousled again.

He smiled miserably. "Be glad you get the chance to make that complaint."

She saw through his smile. She'd hit a raw nerve. Needing to delve deeper in her understanding of him, she said, "Couldn't Ruth have children?"

At once she saw she'd stumbled headlong into no-man's land. Everett wrenched his face away. Without answering, he unfolded himself and walked a distance from her. His hands were jammed in his pockets, pulling his trousers tightly across his hips in the way that always aroused her. His shoulders were pulled forward in a man's instinctive gesture of self-protection.

Jenny followed him, not placing herself at his side but slightly behind. She should let it go, she told herself. She should tell him it was none of her affair and let it go. Instead she slipped her arms about his waist and pressed her cheek to his back.

Sensing her apology, Everett dropped his shoulders. He removed his hands from his pockets and folded them over her arms at his waist. "There was nothing wrong with Ruth."

He faced her suddenly, a sad but purposeful smile on his lips. More like his old self, he pulled a shroud over his unhappiness the way some people made up a bed. In the space of seconds nothing was out of place in his manner—no self-pity, no need for reassurance, nothing except friendship and a need to get on with living.

Not sure if his ability to do this was good or bad, Jenny went with his desire not to talk about it.

"But," he was saying briskly, pulling her to his side and straightening her collar with a casualness that seemed very lonely to her, "that's not your problem. I don't suppose you'd like to race back to the car."

"Are you crazy?"

He shrugged. "I'd win anyway. Let's walk back down together."

He needed the foolishness, she thought. So, perhaps, did she.

She drew back a shoulder. "There's a lot of rubble here to be racing, Everett. You'll break your ankle and then I'll have to carry you back to the hotel."

Grinning, he tweaked a curl at her temple. "Worry about your own ankles, Chicken Little. Unless you're scared, I'll take the rubble outside the wall and you take the smooth part inside. I'll bet you a kiss I get to the car first."

"Betting is for fools and millionaires. And I don't see a smooth part." She considered the car that neither of them could see. "Very well. But I get one minute's head start. Last one down is Felix Unger at a Rolling Stones concert."

From the outset she knew this was a preposterous idea. She nearly twisted her ankle twice before five minutes was out. Where had all this stone come from? She'd have to give it to the old prince, though; he'd once had a quality castle.

She was nearly to the ledge of the second floor when she heard the distant clatter of feet clicking on stone. Everett! How had he managed to get here so quickly?

Frowning, she stopped walking.

The clicking stopped too.

The clever wretch! He had merely skirted the shell and was going to frighten her with one of those boyish

whoops and try and steal his kiss. Well, she'd turn the
tables on him. She would inch back up a few feet and
flatten herself behind the wall of stone. When he
stepped around she'd give him a taste of what it felt like
to be grabbed from behind and goosed in the ribs.

She waited for the soft sounds to begin moving again.
They did and she smiled. The footsteps receded, seem-
ingly higher, and she followed the sound. When it
stopped, she stopped. Her smile disappeared, however,
when she considered the fact that Everett was climbing
much higher than she would have guessed. It wasn't
possible, was it, that she and Everett weren't the only
people wandering about in these ruins?

She peered around the corner of the broken wall.
Nothing. Presently she heard the sounds again—
footsteps, definite footsteps. But now they were behind
her, beyond the opposite wall. They couldn't be Everett's, could they? He couldn't have walked so quickly.
Perhaps there really was someone up here!

After ten minutes of a bizarre hide-and-seek, winding up somewhere far on the west side of the castle,
where the shadows were so long it was nearly dark,
Jenny gazed about herself. She had come much farther
than she had thought. There was no sight of Everett
and no footsteps.

"Everett?"

Nothing.

"Everett! Answer me. Don't play games anymore."

The footsteps immediately sounded behind her
again. Behind her? Whoever or whatever this was was
no longer funny. She was weary of the game now and
more than a little uneasy with her foolishness in not
climbing down while she could see better.

"Everett, I'm ready to stop this. I want to go back."

Nothing. Except the sound of steps. She felt like a
victim in a macabre Edgar Allan Poe tale. Trembling,

feeling the slow drizzle of moisture at the back of her neck and in her palms, Jenny inched around the slab of stone. She had Everett boxed in now, and she was damned ready to tell him what she thought.

As Jenny cautiously eased herself around the extension of gray stone wall, she confronted the footsteps that had cost her many detoured feet and over a half hour of valuable daylight. She screamed as she came face to face with the hairy creature.

Chapter Five

*I*t was unfortunate for Everett, as he looked up to see Jenny shrieking at a goat that was every bit as startled as she was, that he laughed.

Another time, another place, Jenny would have laughed too. But he stood many feet below her, his feet placed solidly and reassuringly upon the ground. Hearing him, peering down, her heart still pounding a frantic tattoo, she hated him with an earnestness that was as real as her lofty predicament.

"How in heaven's name did you get way up there?" he yelled. His handsome head was tipped back; his hands were braced infuriatingly on his hips. "I said race to the car, not wander around on the top of the castle."

Once Jenny realized how absurd she looked, perched high on her cliff, shrilling at some poor innocent beast that had more right to be there than she did, her haughty defensiveness waned.

"Are you afraid to climb down?" he called up. "Do you want me to come up after you?"

What she wanted was for him to go somewhere and leave her alone until she got down. "Don't be ridiculous. I climbed up, didn't I?"

"You climbed up in the daylight, my darling. It'll be dark before you can get down. Don't do that!"

Jenny peered over at the avalanche she'd sent cascading down the ruins. Stones and chunks of mortar clattered until they rolled to an eerie stop at the bottom.

"Stay where you are. I'm coming up."

"I'm all right." She put a silly dramatic bravado in her voice. "I'm a maiden in distress in a wild and untamed land. Isn't the cavalry supposed to arrive now?"

Everett didn't seem to find her joke amusing.

Oh, grief! It was such a stupid, embarrassing child's error—something Stephen or Jeffrey would have done —that Jenny wanted to sit down and cry. All the time she'd been climbing around willy-nilly, she'd been putting herself in a situation where simply losing face would have been a triumph. What woman could present her behind to a man and crawl down a pile of rocks with any degree of dignity?

"Are you all right?" he asked when she didn't start down immediately.

"Do you promise not to laugh?"

"Laugh! Oh, hell, Jenny. Will you get your fanny down here?"

Frustrated, hoping it was too dark for him to see the anatomy in question, plus all her clumsy female contortions, Jenny took a tight hold on her ledge and began inching down over the irregular slope. Getting up had been much less painful than getting back down, she discovered. She scraped a knuckle badly, broke several fingernails, and bruised her kneecap. Halfway down she lost one of her shoes.

"Those are my good Famolares," she wailed.

"Damn the shoe. I've found it. Are you all right?"

No, she wasn't all right!

Her thighs were beginning to ache and the muscles in the calves of her legs quivered. The nerves in the tips of her fingers were screaming from abuse. A recollection of a movie flashed through her mind: mountain climbers on some dangerous mission—was it Michael Caine? —and all that yellow nylon cable and those heavy boots and picks and the man who went crashing over the side. She thought that if she never saw Everett again it would suit her perfectly.

It took her nearly thirty minutes to reach the level of the shadowy castle floor where he waited. And when she finally did reach the ground, only to discover Everett blithely sitting on a rock, holding her shoe, rash tears scalded her eyelids.

Everett made his worst mistake when he tried to examine the knuckle she sucked on.

"Leave me alone!" she cried at him, and snatched her shoe from his hand.

"You little goose. I told you to go to the car. Didn't you ever learn that this is your right hand and this is your left? This"—he pointed up with his thumb—"is up, and this . . . well, I guess you figured out down all by yourself."

She hit him in the center of his chest with her shoe.

Everett grabbed at her when she struck, but she spun quickly away.

The whole incident hadn't been that easy on him, he thought with considerable irritation. He'd suffered his own private distress when he hadn't found Jenny at the car. Now, to be made the villain for something not remotely his fault, sent a spurt of self-pity welling up inside him.

He caught a handful of her jacket as she whirled. "Maybe I should have left you out here all night by yourself."

Jenny knocked his hands off her jacket. She stomped toward the car, which was a vague hulk in the darkness. "Maybe you should have."

With a look of exasperation that was lost on her, Everett swore a blistering oath. Watching her tromp to the car, her hips flexing with such provocativeness beneath her slacks, set his teeth on edge. He'd been fantasizing ever since she'd walked out of that bathroom. He couldn't make a move on this woman. It would be disastrous. Part of him was appalled at the idea. Then why were his hands trembling so badly that he balled them into fists? What was happening to all his famous Black cool, as Ruth had often thrown in his face when he kept to his own room and spoke in monosyllables?

He caught up with her in three strides. He jerked her about with a grasp of her shoulders. "Maybe a cold night with nature would do something to improve your temper, my darling!"

"Maybe it would help yours!"

Her head snapped back when he gave her a little shake.

He looked down at her, limp in his arms. Her silence had its own voice, accusing him of hurting her before, of marrying the wrong woman. Suddenly her silence became the lonely vacancies of his whole life—Everett the answerable man, not the forgivable youth. The silence of his house in Boston was mocking him and the void of the children's bedrooms. And now her. He couldn't bear the pain of that silence any longer!

As easily as lifting a feather, he grabbed her beneath

her buttocks and scooped her off the ground. One arm clamped her spine in a breath-crushing vise, the other slammed the bones of her pelvis hard against his.

"Take your hands off me!" she yelped.

He spoke through his teeth. "I know what I promised you back in Atlanta, so you'd better tell me no, Jenny, before I do this."

"No." Her eyes grew big with her intuitive woman's fear. She knew what he was thinking, and she leaned backward.

He was already bending over her, following her mouth.

"No!"

She gave a faint little cry and struggled to drag her arms free of his rough embrace, but he caught the wrist of her free arm and twisted it behind her. Heat burned his neck now, and his throat was dry. Everett thought, as he forcibly pinned her against him, that she had never been so irresistible. She was fighting him with the strength of a strapping boy. He could hardly hold her, and the more he tried, the more determined he became to have her—all of her.

His lips collided with the curve of her neck and shoulder. "Be still, Jenny," he groaned. "Please be still."

There was a certain shredding of his pride couched in his words, and Jenny's stillness came with the abruptness of cold thrown upon hot. She ceased her struggling, her breasts heaving against him as she tried to breathe, her eyes begging him not to open up the past again.

Everett didn't see her melancholy plea. He only felt her slender rigidity melting against him. He bent over her again. "So sweet," he mumbled, searching for her lips, finding them with short, hard kisses. His tongue plunged through the barrier of her teeth. "Sweet . . . sweet . . . lady."

She didn't fight as he devoured her mouth, his tongue darting, assaulting hers, demanding with an urgency that bordered on ruthlessness. One of her arms lifted, dropped, then lifted again to twine about his neck. She was still clutching her shoe, and that arm, too, draped itself delicately upon his shoulder.

Without relinquishing her lips, Everett caught her up in his arms like a baby and walked with her to the car. Her head was tipped back over the curve of his shoulder. Her other shoe was dangling precariously from her toes. By some acrobatic feat, tasting her endlessly, he managed to open the back door of the car. Ducking his head, he fell with her to the seat.

"I'd forgotten, Jenny." He relished the feel of her beneath him with an intensity of arousal he'd thought was dead to him. "I'd forgotten how good you are."

She felt the mixture of desire and reluctance in him. "You can't even consider doing this, Everett."

"That's all I've considered since I saw you that day in Atlanta."

"Listen to me."

"I came back home, Jenny, thinking I'd find you all safe and unavailable. I thought I wouldn't have to be reminded of what a fool I'd been to leave you."

"Everett—"

"And you turned out to be more beautiful, more . . . everything. Dammit, Jenny, why couldn't you have gotten hard and hateful and ugly?"

"Oh, Everett!"

Jenny knew him well. The years hadn't changed him that much. His hungry caresses were only the tip of the iceberg. And the backseat of a car wouldn't stop him from making love to her. She wondered if he hated the thoughts of her making love to Ray. She wondered if she would ever hear him say she was the only woman who could make him want to marry again. But when he fit himself between her legs, she knew he wasn't thinking of Ray. She pushed against his shoulders, telling him no, but his motion was steady and urging.

"Let me, Jenny," he pleaded softly. "Let me love you again. Just once more before I die."

"You said you wouldn't. . . . You lied to me."

"I didn't lie." His mouth continued to explore her face, her neck, her ears. He nipped the point of her chin. "I was wrong to ever promise it."

"This is wrong."

"It was never wrong. Not for us. How did I ever lose you, Jenny?"

His nibbling at her breast through her blouse sent electrifying currents through her. She felt her own nails burying into the swell of his biceps.

"Am I going to pay the rest of my life for losing you, Jenny?"

Jenny knew that forcing his head up would only inflame him more. Everett was flicking her buttons loose with astounding skill. He seemed to know exactly how to negotiate the clip of her bra. It snapped in his fingers and spilled her breasts. They gleamed starkly white in the darkness. They both stared at them, Everett catching his breath in a short, ragged gasp.

She tried to cover them with her hands. "Oh, no. Don't look at me."

Not understanding, Everett attempted to pull her hands away. "You're perfect, darling."

"Oh, God, please." She had never conceptualized the defeat of a moment such as this.

"Jen, what could you possibly . . ."

"I've . . . I . . . oh, I've had babies, Everett!" She squeezed her eyes shut.

"But—"

"The scars . . . don't look at me."

Slowly Everett pried loose her hands from holding the pale, rounded curves.

At his mercy, Jenny turned her face away and hid behind her arm. From the pink tips of her breasts extended fine, delicately drawn lines of silver-white, now so faint they were scarcely visible. They faded into the smooth swell that, because she was small, was as high and firm as always. Jenny remembered how he'd adored her breasts before, when they'd thrust in their proud, eighteen-year-old impudence. She couldn't believe that Everett could find her beautiful now. Every scar was to her an unwanted price she'd paid for growing older and becoming a mother. She groaned with inexpressible misery.

Bending, and with infinite tenderness, Everett cupped one of her breasts and kissed the tiny scars, above and beneath. He nudged the nipple with the tip of his tongue. It stirred and grew taut against his mouth.

"Oh, love," he breathed with impulsive honesty, "they should have been my babies. These scars should have been because of me."

She had thought it abstractly herself, but the vast disloyalty of it, the crime of it, had never let her actually form it into a concept.

Soundlessly she began to cry. "I'm sorry," she said in a hushed, very private desolation.

Everett suddenly felt as if some of his bones were missing. The terrible depths of her frightened him. It also awakened something to life that had succumbed so slowly, he wasn't even aware of its passing.

The women in his past, after his marriage had begun to crumble, had always been a certain type of woman, never anyone free to become emotionally involved with, never anyone he would consider for more than an occasional encounter. After a few years he'd learned he could never father children. The mental tricks he'd learned to play upon himself were as varied and as lavish as his regrets. In time he'd come to forget they were tricks. Now he was reminded of them, and he remembered where he'd come from. This woman had brought it all back, this small, lovely woman who wept over her scars of childbearing when his scars were by far the most deep and the most deadly. Oh, God, the truth! Yes, he'd wanted roots and the ties of marriage. And he wanted Jenny. Now, holding her, he didn't know if he'd ever stopped wanting her through the years. But he was terrified of both—of his inabilities as a man and of loving her.

Gradually, like his sanity returning, his passion faded. It began to drift intangibly out of reach until he smoothed back her curls from her face and kissed the moistness of her lashes, letting her know the danger of the moment was past.

Jenny blinked mistily at him. His sadness was an indefinable shadow down the sides of his mouth.

"Promise me something," he said huskily.

"What?"

"That you'll never say those words to me again. Not about that."

"You don't understand."

"*You* don't understand. To me you're the most beautiful woman I've ever known. No, don't interrupt. What was between Ruth and me was different. She was a beautiful woman. She still is. But she never felt the need to be sorry for anything." He shook his head. "And you, of all people, shouldn't feel sorry. Not to me, darling innocent. Not to me."

"I always wanted to be pretty for you, Everett."

His guilt was monstrous. He turned his face away—a grim profile. "God, you make me despise myself!"

Her hands lifted to the sides of his face. The stubble of new beard was scratchy against her palms. In her need to soothe his scars she forgot her own. She forced him to look at her.

"Everett, we did some foolish things. For a while I thought I couldn't go on without you. But my life filled up. Nothing in real life works out like you plan it. It's no one's fault, really. You learn to settle for something else, to go on."

Still covering her with his body, he resettled his weight and lay for long, silent minutes, his cheek pillowed upon the space between her breasts, his palm unconsciously shaped about her ribs.

"There were women," he said quietly. "I wasn't faithful to her."

"You don't have to tell me that."

"I've always regretted it. I've thought if I'd been faithful, I could've looked back and said I'd at least fulfilled my part of the bargain." He sighed.

"Were you terribly unhappy?"

"Not for the reason you think. I wanted to prove something, that if I couldn't be a father, I could be a prolific lover, I guess. I don't know."

Jenny threaded her fingers through the hair that grew long at his neckline. There it tended to curl, not nearly so rebellious as the rest. She didn't know what to say to comfort him.

"You don't have to answer this if you don't want to," he said, hesitating, "but after Martin died, did you . . ."

She knew his arousal had abated now, partly from her words and partly from his own self-doubts. But her own had only banked; it was secretly smoldering, capable of bursting into heated flames. Deep inside pulsed a thick, needful ache. She had always been too slow for her men, hadn't she?

She shifted her legs. "I never had an affair, Everett."

He braced his weight on his hands and stared down at her. "But eight years, Jenny . . ."

She smiled faintly, her eyes closing in spite of herself. "Women have ways, Everett, just like men, of making do."

"Well, woman"—he smiled and clipped the front of her bra. He began buttoning her blouse—"I'm taking you back and putting you to bed. Tomorrow is time enough for me to make a fool of myself again."

Not a fool, she thought, a flesh-and-blood man that she loved more than she thought possible.

Jenny couldn't sleep. For hours she lay in the dark, her eyes heavy-lidded but awake. She tried not to think about the long shadow stretched full length beside her. Everett's breathing was slow and steady. Carefully she turned on her side to watch the dim outline of his chest as it fell, rose, fell again.

How long had she lain here, unable to soothe the solitary woman's need, the empty aching? If she were home alone she could ease it, or cry, or get up and read a book, or make a sandwich. Now she could do nothing but listen to him breathe and imagine herself doing. . . . She touched her breasts, feeling them swell, making her ache even worse. She tried to remember the exact way she'd felt when he had thrust against her through her slacks. She imagined him buried inside her, her hands fitting upon those lean, muscular hips. But mostly she imagined his need, the lengths that it would drive him, that she was the only one who could satisfy it and him telling her that.

A quiver shot through her as if she had touched an exposed wire. To hell with this!

Slipping off the bed, she padded silently to the window. Somewhere a car door slammed. Some tourist as sleepless as she, she supposed. Far in the distance a dog barked. Did it belong to the eel farmer who'd poled his boat in such disdain? Was the farmer, with all his sun-browned gauntness and his creeping old age, more blessed than she because he was wrapped in the arms of his wife, sleeping a healthy and untroubled slumber?

Jenny didn't turn around when she heard Everett dragging on his trousers. She waited until she felt his hands upon the waist of her terry robe. The easy weight of them made her want to collapse. *Touch me*, she begged inside her head. *I take back everything I said. Hold me, love me. I need you.*

"I couldn't sleep," she said after a time. She grimaced when she felt him shiver. "Go back to bed. You'll catch your death."

"That expression went out before you were born."

She hesitated, felt his own hesitation. "I guess I'm just an old-fashioned girl."

"Old-fashioned is bad?"

"It's inconvenient. I don't have affairs, and I worry because I don't look like the girls in *Playboy* magazine."

Everett released her. Stepping back, he dragged his fingers through his hair. "Why don't you say what you're really thinking, Jenny? That you're old-fashioned because you still hold out for marriage? That you wish I felt about marriage the same as you?"

The silence was as long and drafty as the room, the truth as stinging as his nerve to say it so baldly.

"What I think is," she said, moving away from him to touch one of the plastic daffodils on the low table, "that it was a mistake for me ever to come here."

Everett felt cornered and uncertain of what to do next. "I'm a man who learns my lessons, Jenny. I wish you could understand that. I learned the hard way."

Why wouldn't he change his mind? He was so sensitive and kind. Surely he could change. Surely she could *make* him change.

"Then we've reached an impasse, haven't we?" she said, head bent, eyes staring at nothing. "Me set in my old-fashioned ways and you having learned your lessons?"

He shrugged. "We could both give a little."

She laughed softly, bitterly. "It's always the woman who ends up giving the most, Everett. I don't need that."

"But you do need, Jenny. You need me. You've got a long fuse, sweet lady, and it's burning right now, slowly but surely."

Unable to believe his nerve to say such a thing, Jenny whirled. Her robe was a cloudy swirl in the darkness. She moved to the bed. She snatched a pillow and held it to herself as if it were plated armor. Her hands were shaking and she tried to stop them.

"You're crude, Everett. You're vulgar."

Everett lowered himself to his side of the bed and let his back slump in a curve. The lean flesh at his waist folded upon itself. Jenny wanted to go to him, to wrap her arms about his back and press her cheek against it. She remained where she was—trembling, not from fear but because what he'd said was true.

"You're wrong," she insisted.

"No, I'm not."

"Yes."

"No!"

He said nothing.

Finally, for there was nothing else to do, she flung

the pillow against the plain wooden headboard. Keeping on her robe, she stretched out, dragged the blanket to her chin, and covered her eyes with her arm. She felt him stand, heard him remove his trousers, and knew when he crawled into bed. The awareness of him lying beside her was like an injection that left her helplessly immobile. The scent of him—his hands, his hair, his body—made her want to admit the truth, all of it that she knew.

"Why did you think I was lying?" she asked from behind her arm.

"Do you really want me to answer that question?"

At length she said, "Yes."

Everett pulled up on his elbow. Jenny drew her arm away and looked at him in puzzlement.

"Kneel down on the bed, Jenny," he said softly.

"Everett—"

"You asked me to answer it."

She did as he said, sitting on her heels, her eyes never leaving his.

"Now take off your gown."

Shocks of pleasure shot through her like gold wires. Warm liquid response made her go boneless.

"No." She shook her head.

"And if I said you've punished me enough for my mistake, would you take it off?"

Her understanding bent her low upon herself. For long, condemning moments she lay folded, kneeling before the shrine of her own past hurt. She heard him drag himself up to lean against the headboard as if he was waiting and would continue to wait.

He didn't say he was sorry for opening her eyes so heartlessly, and she didn't expect it. When she lifted her head, her chin held at a proud, audacious angle, the moonlight that chased across the room caught the crest of her cheekbones. The room didn't even feel chilly anymore. It hadn't been her scars that had made her feel less than beautiful, she knew; it was fearing to love without the sure, steel promises of marriage.

Where did the trust begin? Feeling that if she failed herself now she would never have the courage to dare again, Jenny let her robe slide off her shoulders to drape about her hips. She drew a strap of her gown over one pale shoulder, then the other. Still locked in his relentless gaze, she drew the shimmering gown to the column of her waist and stilled: an offering in an ethereal, spellbinding ceremony.

Only then did Everett's eyes move over her. His lips were parted slightly as he lay captivated by a beauty he had never expected. When he smiled, Jenny was shocked at her quick elation. She felt suddenly vibrant and eager, breathless with dependence upon his desire for her.

With an unfamiliar aggression that made time stop completely, she drew herself upon the length of his body. Low upon her hips, the gown twisted between them. She lifted one hand to the headboard, then the other. Then, her back arched in a high ellipse that began and ended with him, she touched his lips with the tip of her breast. He made no sudden moves, only enough to take it slowly into his mouth. She saw his lashes flutter closed and heard the groan tear in his throat. The feel of her own weight lowering onto his lent her the courage to give herself up to it. She was burning when, seconds later, he turned her onto her back.

He looked down at her with glowing, slate-blue eyes. "That was what you wanted."

"Yes."

His mouth was voracious and hard upon hers. She

reached between them and felt for him, whimpering with pleasure at proof of his need. Her breath caught as he rolled off her. His briefs were the color of dark wine, and banded at the top of long, symmetrical legs. She flinched when his larger hand closed over hers—knowing, steady—and placed it upon him.

"I don't know if I'm that honest," she whispered, knowing what he wanted.

"It's all right if you're not. None of us tells all the truth. I want terribly to love you, Jenny," he said in a voice she hardly recognized. "You know that, don't you?"

She closed her eyes as she voiced her logic. "Don't call it love."

"What else can I call it?"

"Call it sex."

"Oh, darling, it's so much more than that."

"You said to be honest."

Their words came with difficulty now; even breathing came with difficulty. Her fingers seemed on fire as they lay along the waist of his briefs.

"Then be honest," he whispered. "Do what you want to do. I won't get you pregnant."

"I didn't mean—"

It didn't matter what she'd meant. Her own words had said not to call it love. But that was because he'd been hurt by an unloving marriage. For her it was more than before. God help her—much, much more. Knowing exactly what she was doing, hoping somewhere in the secret recesses of her mind that history wasn't repeating itself, Jenny tugged at the scrap of fabric about his middle.

Everett possessed the most sensitive hands she had ever imagined. He drew her upon him and dispensed with the film of gown in one swift movement. She lay weightless upon him as he fit her legs to his sides. Capturing her mouth, teaching her to trust by caresses of her hips, the lines fashioning the outsides of her thighs, he lifted himself up to find her. When he did, their eyes locked with a mutual tenacity to know the closest touching possible, he reached very deeply, very powerfully. She clung to him, moving against him with an exquisite mindlessness that drifted back and forth.

Eyes widening, hardly recognizing her small, surprised sound, Jenny buried her fingernails into his shoulders. She shuddered with the completion of a quest that had begun hours earlier; her face searched for the safety of his neck. Everett refused her the serenity of rest. Again he hurled her out into space, and again she groped for something solid to cling to. She was covered with a sheen that smelled of her perfume and her own fiery passion. She tried to think logically and found lucidity pierced with a silvery spear once again. She fell heavily against him, shaking her head and whispering, "No more, no more."

She lay beside him in silence for a time, comfortably floating, her cheek resting against the ridge of his knuckles. His hand found the bare curve of her hip. "What're you thinking?" he asked drowsily, his voice thick with arousal.

"About the boundless energy of that hand."

He smiled and let his hand, as if in a reply to her accusation, slide across her waist. Her muscles quivered. It slowly crept lower to search for her, to stroke.

Jenny stuffed her face into the side of his shoulder. "Don't do that," she mumbled.

"Why not? You're ready."

"I'm all loved up."

"A woman's never loved up."

"I can't do it again."

He rolled over to face her.

She kept her eyes closed. "At least this way," she said, "I can console myself that it was . . . a slip. To do it again would be . . ."

Everett wrapped his arms about her. "In the first place it wasn't a slip. It was a deliberate expression between two people. You can't end something like that, Jenny. You can't turn it off so easily."

Jenny's eyes were clear as she leaned back to stare at him. "You know the way I am. Probably better in some ways than I do myself. I was telling you the truth when I said I couldn't have an open-ended relationship, Everett. It's not in me."

She lay lightly in his arms, warm, half dreaming. Without warning, Everett reached between them. He smiled at her short, harsh gasp when he slipped his fingers inside her. She slumped against him, thinking how unfair he was to prove his point this way.

"I'm not asking for an open-ended anything," he muttered into the shell of her ear. All his concentration was centered on her smallest response.

"Do you know what you make me feel?" he asked when she moaned softly and began to move restlessly against his hand.

"Ohh," she whimpered, twisting.

"I want to be everything for you, Jenny. Nothing of myself."

Her back arched slightly as he knelt beside her waist. He kissed the silky whiteness of her belly. Jenny wanted to capture his head in her hands, to stop him from going further, but she didn't.

She took a quick breath. "We should go to sleep."

"We should do a lot of things," he said as he shifted so that he could see all of her.

Being studied so intimately was unnerving, even

though her love for him was crowded to the front of her consciousness. Meaning to move beyond Everett's reach, she grew enchanted with the sight of his lithe, tanned body kneeling beside hers. That was her first experience of viewing herself from a far distance. He was changing her, she thought. He was doing things to her that Martin had rarely done. She couldn't go back to what she was before, could she? Not ever.

Everett ignored her protests as he filled his hands with her hips. Lifting her and lowering his head at the same instant, he touched her.

Jenny couldn't speak. She caught her lip in her teeth. His eyes fastened to hers and held them as undeniably, as irrevocably, as the sensations that began to spiral inside her. She couldn't look away and she couldn't deny him. She could only react to the heightening tension he was building, tangling her fingers in his hair until, at the last possible moment, he straightened. He pulled upon her and carefully filled her. It was hard and quick for him, as if the waiting had been more than he could bear. And then came the end, at least temporarily, to her aching emptiness of half a lifetime.

"Come to Boston with me," he begged her later in the darkness of early morning. Sleep was overtaking them both. "Come to Boston when we're finished here. Live with me, and we can work it out, whatever it takes. We can't let this end between us."

For a time Jenny had forgotten the realities of the world, her own family, her standards. She didn't know what to tell him. She kept hearing his words while she grew aware of her own body. He had loved her insatiably; she was sore from containing him. He'd come to the brink of commitment and pulled back without any talk of forever. Live with him? Work it out? How could she work anything out? He wouldn't marry her, and she couldn't even conceive of marrying Ray now. No, she couldn't live with Everett. What would be left but to end it?

"You haven't given me an answer," he said drowsily.

She fit against his back and nestled her head into her pillow. Her words fell breathily upon his shoulder blades. "What answer could I possibly give you, Everett?"

"If it's your family, those things can be coped with. It's not as if we don't know how to play games with the public."

"My sons are hardly the public." He hadn't even said he loved her!

"Hell, Jenny, what's so great about marriage? We'd have everything but the little piece of paper. I've had the piece of paper, and so have you. Would you rather have it or what we've had the last hours?"

What she wanted was both.

"Is it the commitment? There's no woman for me anymore except you. How could I ever touch another woman?"

She had no doubts about that, or at least she thought she didn't. "It's a matter of . . ." Would he understand, this man who'd grown up watching the cruelties of his father? "It's a matter of correctness, Everett. I'm liberated in a sense, but not that way. And it's not really what people would say."

"Correctness!"

"Yes, correctness. There are a few correct people left, who are not out killing people or stealing or lying—"

"Or living together without being married."

"Yes!"

He sighed with a complete resignation to his failure.

He reached behind him and pulled her as close as it was possible for her to be. He let his hand lay on her thigh. "Later," he said wearily. "We'll talk about this again."

"My answer will still be the same."

"Later," he said and yawned.

"Later," she answered, thinking, *Why can't I break your heart?*

Chapter Six

𝒮ome things in life were so enormous, Jenny thought as she stared down at Ruth Black from the stairway, that they were impossible to reconcile. Who would have guessed, even in the wildest explosion of imagination, that she would have come face-to-face with Everett's ex-wife halfway around the world?

There was no question in Jenny's mind who the woman was. It was the way she stood, perhaps, in the center of the lobby with three casually dressed men who were traveling with her. She was blond, quite beautiful, her unlit cigarette dangling from between her gloved fingers in a weary, expensive, cared-for look, and she was surveying the room with an expression of elegant boredom. Her head turned leisurely as Jenny and Everett descended the stairs. She held a pose as she spotted them. For one brief second her eyes were totally all-seeing.

She knows what we've done! Jenny thought with a

flash of shrill instinct. Did women possess some inborn ESP, some innate radar, that enabled them to sense when they'd been loved by the same man? Was there a look? A sign? With or without it the woman knew everything.

Jenny paused on the step and reached back for Everett without turning. "Everett?"

The quick intake of breath behind Jenny only confirmed what she already knew deep in her bones.

"I'll be damned," Everett said, bereft of his usual calm. "Ruth."

Then, with the self-protective device Nature instills in order for one to cope, Jenny's mind cut itself off from reality for a moment or two.

"This will be all right," Everett was reassuring her from behind her shoulder.

But his words meant nothing. For those seconds to Jenny it was the same as when Major Donovan had sat in her living room, his big hands folded upon his knees, and told her that Martin was dead. She'd known everything that was happening, but all she could focus on was how one side of his collar had slipped free of his uniform and was pinched haphazardly toward his neck.

All Jenny could see now, looking at Ruth, was the cleaning man who pushed his broom up behind her and stopped, waiting. Noticing him, Ruth Black glanced at her case sitting on the floor beside her feet. She made no move to pick it up, but rather placed her cigarette between her lips and began removing her gloves. In an almost ludicrous standoff the cleaning man shifted his weight, clamped the handle of his broom beneath one arm, and didn't move. Ruth lifted her fingernails in a leisurely inspection. In those half-real seconds Jenny suffered a suffocating compulsion to protect herself and Everett from this woman.

"Everett?" From across the lobby Ruth waved her gloves at them. "Everett!"

Jenny felt Everett's hand firmly reassuring upon her elbow. She was laboriously involved with her feet, the task of placing them one after another until she reached the bottom of the stairs. She must pretend that she was a woman of sophistication, she told herself. She must, by some veil of poise, smile with a face that said she did not feel guilty.

Without a passing thought for the cleaning man, Ruth stooped for the case at her feet and moved toward Everett with an effortless model's glide.

The three men, unmindful of Ruth's tiny drama with the hotel employee, showed recognition of Everett with various degrees of gesturing and talking between themselves. They ambled behind Ruth, their arms draped with coats and suitcases and garment bags.

"The men are members of my staff," Everett explained quickly when they reached the landing. "They're nice men. They would never trespass into my private life without being invited."

"But she—"

"I had no idea. Leave Ruth to me. She can't hurt you, darling."

Was that supposed to comfort her after seeing Ruth's power play with a faceless entity who meant absolutely nothing? Jenny's fingernails cut into the palms of her hands.

"Divorced men have all kinds of built-in problems, I'm afraid. Ruth is one of mine. Stay close to me."

In a defensive and quite futile gesture, Jenny touched the cuff of his jacket. "I hate this," she said bitterly, and matched her steps to his.

Ruth laughed when they were near enough to talk without shouting.

"Everett, darling, we had no idea you were at the hotel." She was aware of her beauty and flaunted it as if it were something she was entitled to without question. "I spent the night with some woman from Norfolk, Virginia. Her husband's in the Navy. Darling, you look positively exhausted."

During the first seconds that Ruth smiled at Jenny, Jenny saw what Everett had been attracted to in her—a charm, an irresistible warmth that could reach out and embrace one. He hadn't exaggerated her beauty. Her eyes were perhaps the most striking thing about her with their deep emerald brilliance. Her face was oval and slender, the type that looked good with any hairstyle. She was in her thirties, but her complexion was made up so well, she would have easily passed for Jenny's own age, except for the world-weary disdain that she wore like the fabulous Ernst Strauss suit she had on.

Her warmth drained away almost immediately, like an elusive handful of sand through fingers, leaving nothing but an impression of lovely, smiling distaste.

Inconspicuously placing himself between Ruth and Jenny, more a shifting of attitude than physical movement, Everett answered his ex-wife with a toneless calm that was the exact opposite of what Jenny expected.

"And you look lovely, Ruth, as always." He turned away from her and, with a complete reversal of manner, eagerly shook the hand of one of the men. "Dave, am I glad to see you!"

Dave clapped an arm about Everett's shoulders in the affection of an old, much revered friend. He was forty, Jenny figured, but she surmised that by his hands, not his face. He had a ruddy complexion and a vast, well-preserved body. He possessed the tranquil melancholy of genius, and his clothes were very untidy.

But his gray eyes were piercing. They didn't fit his face; they were the eyes of an old man.

"I thought Germany would have your ears pinned back by now, boy," laughed Dave. "What d'you do? Cast spells?"

"You think I'm a warlock, do you?" Everett grinned at the other two men, who were waiting to be acknowledged. "Hamburg tells me they're not only going to donate one of their top men, they're going to throw in a spectroscope too. What d'you think, Simon? Black magic, eh?"

Everyone laughed. A private joke, Jenny assumed. There was much about Everett's life she didn't know. Were they all looking at her and thinking the same thing?

The arm Everett slipped about Jenny's waist was unobtrusively possessive. He drew her into the group with a minimum of awkwardness. "Jenny, this is Dave Lytton, a man without whom I would be up to my armpits in various and sundry muck."

When Dave Lytton smiled at her over his handshake, Jenny had the feeling that he knew exactly how awkward she felt. There was something about Dave's gallantry that won her immediately.

"Half of Europe calls Everett 'The Scrounger,' Mrs. Howard," Dave explained. "They like to see him come, but after he's gone they discover he's talked them out of hundreds of thousands of dollars' worth of equipment. They stand there scratching their heads while he rides off into the sunset to build these things he builds."

Jenny summoned all the resources she had stored from her dealings with Bartlett Street and Alan Kendall and half a dozen others. Brightly she said, "Cowpokes who ride off into the sunset are notoriously long-lived, Mr. Lytton. They always return to fight the same battle and the same Indians again."

"And they always get the girl," Ruth threw in with only a trace of rancor. "Is your charming friend a reporter, Everett?"

The cheerful surface of the moment was shattered. Everyone knew she wasn't a reporter. Everett's fury flashed and was swept under control so swiftly that Jenny's smile hardly had time to stiffen on her lips. Lord in heaven, don't let there be a scene!

Dave Lytton stepped in quickly. "Ruth invented the surprise attack," he said, effectively switching the attention to himself.

And then it was gone—the discomfort that was like the sharp jab of a needle and withdrawn. Except antagonism lingered in Dave's eyes when he looked at Ruth. The dislike, Jenny saw, was an old one. She guessed that the man's protection of Everett was instinctive by now.

In his capacity as ranking executive, though without appearing to be laying down the ground rules, Everett neatly dispensed with any questions about Jenny before they could be asked. His manner, unruffled yet underlaid with an authoritative hint of toughness, warned that Jenny was strictly off limits.

"Mrs. Howard will be doing some of the internal work," he explained succinctly. Then, channeling their interest elsewhere, he addressed a slender man with a narrow black beard and a great nose—a computer expert, Everett said. "I wasn't sure I'd see you on this one, Simon. I'm glad you could make it on such short notice. Josh, I've got a dozen questions about the plant foundations."

The tallest man of the three, Josh McClellan, a big, beefy man whose Viking's mane of blond hair flowed to his collar, was a civil engineer from Akron, Ohio. "Can you believe this flood?" he boomed with a voice like a moose, and fished for a cigar. "Four major bridges out. Fifteen thousand people having to be evacuated. What's the cubic feet per second, have you heard? Anybody got a light?"

"A hundred fifty to two hundred thousand," answered Everett, all business. "A lot of water, gentlemen."

Ruth fluttered her very long, very red fingernails in a wave. "I'm happy to meet you, Jennifer Howard. My husband—pardon me, my ex-husband—is indispensable, you know." She gestured at the way the men fell into shop talk. "Once they begin working, you could go dancing or wash your hair for all they'd know."

Feeling literally dowdy in her sweater and skirt and boots, Jenny caught Everett's knowing look. He smiled. If she loved Everett, if she wanted him—to love, to marry, to anything—she would have to cope with Ruth in one form or another. She drew comfort from Everett's subtle protectiveness and let Ruth carry the conversation, something Ruth seemed to do without much effort.

Ruth pulled an attractive pout across her face. "We've just spent a half hour trying to get you on the phone at the lab, Everett. The office in Boston told me you flew over day before yesterday." Her green eyes flicked toward Jenny. "I was in Vienna with Aunt Sib when I heard the news. I'll do what I can to help. As a senior member of the board, I don't want our stock dropping on the market any more than's necessary, naturally."

"Naturally," murmured Everett with only a ripple of mockery.

"So you're in interiors, too, Jennifer." Ruth's smile slashed redly. "How coincidental. And how fortunate for you, too, Everett, considering the job at hand. Now you can do your work with your past and your present close at hand."

Another awkward beat fell, embarrassing the men, except for Josh McClellan, who was busily chewing his cigar and wadding his *Sports Illustrated* into the front pocket of his Windbreaker.

Everett gestured for Jenny to precede him toward the door that opened toward the cafe beside the market. The only evidence of his anger was the surge of tension in his arm that lightly circled Jenny's back. And his hand that trembled over her ribs.

"I think she hates me," Jenny mumbled through unmoving lips.

His voice was dry. "It isn't you she hates."

Ruth called after him. "You two were on your way to breakfast, weren't you?"

"As it happens," Everett tossed over his shoulder. "You're welcome to come. Simon, Josh, Dave—all of you. It's a working breakfast."

Ruth swung her case over her shoulder by one finger and strode quickly to lead the way. Dave, falling into step with Jenny, made her feel he was protecting her flank.

The scientific wizard, as he caught up with Everett, brushed at his suit. It looked as if he'd slept in it for three days. Then, as if he gave up trying to restore any order to himself, he turned and began walking backward so he could see Everett's face.

"This is the damnedest town, Everett. Have you noticed the goats? They're everywhere."

Jenny didn't dare show a flicker of emotion when Everett's amused look bounced off her own.

"Goats? Can't say as I have," he drawled, laughter deep in his chest. "But that's not to say they aren't around. Up in the hills, I expect."

* * *

Some twenty minutes later Jenny found herself sitting across from Ruth, apprehensively stirring a cup of black coffee as Everett became the razor-sharp organizer she'd never seen before.

"Is Harrison coming over from Bell laboratories?" Dave was asking.

"Ah, Dave," murmured Ruth. "Good old Dave. Always worrying." She replaced her cup onto her saucer and lit a cigarette. She blew smoke toward the ceiling like Marlene Dietrich.

Everett ignored her. "I talked to him. He said it would be a few days before he could cut loose, but he'd come."

Simon talked around his eggs. "I guess all the equipment's ruined?"

"Yes."

"Oh, damn. That sweet computer."

"Afraid so," Everett said. He hadn't touched his breakfast. He was working on his third cup of coffee. "I'll talk to the insurance people."

Ruth ground out her cigarette. "I told you we should have built that place a mile farther from the river."

"We went all over that, Ruth. It would have cost us six extra months just to get the roads and the utilities."

"And now you'll wait six months for repairs."

"It's over and done. A freak accident no one could have predicted."

Tongue in cheek, Ruth cut her arresting eyes toward Jenny. "Aren't they all, darling?"

Jenny dropped her spoon. The three members of the staff shifted uncomfortably in their chairs, even Josh. Everett smiled at Ruth with what Jenny suspected was a dangerous smile. Not a fraction of his control appeared to shift. Without a word he unrolled a cylinder of plans that Josh had brought with him. Smoothing them across the top of the table, pointing to a place in particular, he began questioning the civil engineer. "What d'you think, Josh? If you had to guess, sight unseen, will the plumbing have to go? You put it in, you should know."

What did it take with Everett? Jenny wondered. The woman was deliberately needling him, yet he took and took and took.

Dave Lytton retrieved Jenny's spoon and placed it beyond her cup. He smiled warmly when he caught her eye. He'd unzipped his leather jacket, and he reached into it for a piece of chewing gum. When he offered her a piece she shook her head.

"You've known Everett a long time," she mused as they both watched everyone bending over the drawings.

He folded his gum wrapper in a half-dozen creases. "We do go back a way, Everett and I," he said, and counted with separate beats of his arm as he listed them. "Let's see, we had malaria together in Nigeria, got hijacked together in South Africa, and now we're going to shovel through a flood in Spain."

He wiped his hand across his mouth. "Would you like to walk? They'll be at this for a while."

She nodded.

Without saying anything to the rest, they strolled onto the street. It was bustling about with dented pickups bringing produce to the cafe and to the market. Natives were yelling directions to strangers with much shrugging and waving of arms. The sky was coolly blue, as if it couldn't be worried with trivial mankind.

She hugged herself.

Dave Lytton interrupted her musing. "He works miracles sometimes. He's gotten awards and commendations he never tells anyone about."

"Really?" Her surprise was genuine.

Dave drew a fingertip across his upper lip as if considering his words. "I'm going to tell you something, Jennifer. May I call you Jennifer? Actually I generally go through this little ritual for the new people. I've found it saves a lot of headaches."

Jenny met his directness with a questioning brow.

"Especially if Ruth's around. She loves to tell the new people about me. I learned a long time ago that I was protected only if I got my licks in first."

"You sound mysterious, Mr. Lytton."

"Dave." He wrapped his chewed gum in an old wrapper and folded a fresh piece into his mouth. He cocked a gray-streaked brow. "I'm trying to quit smoking," he explained rather sheepishly. "And I'm not mysterious, really, just practical. I used to be a surgeon, you see. A good surgeon. When Everett and I became friends, I was serving a term in prison."

Jenny stopped walking altogether. Telling this might be an oft-repeated habit with Dave, but it obviously wasn't an easy thing for him.

He chewed his gum without looking at her.

"*Euthanasia* is the nice word for it. And I won't go into it or my reasons for it. That's between God and myself. Anyway, Everett gave me a job when I got out of the penitentiary. He's taken a lot of flak because of me. A couple of newspapers have really come down hard on him. No matter how many times I've wanted to pull out, he wouldn't let me."

He turned and gazed down with eyes that were strangely unsettling. "That's about the size of it. Just wanted you to hear the straight of it from me."

Hearing such a damaging confession from a man she didn't know was a unique experience for Jenny. She understood completely why he'd told her, and she understood his protectiveness for Everett and his antagonism toward Ruth. She doubted that Dave could guess how this knowledge affected her as a woman. Her love for Everett—that feeling she'd tried to deny, to ignore, and finally to destroy—only deepened with the recounting of this story.

"Oh, Dave," she said softly, "life can be so cruel on one side and so unbearably wonderful on the other."

"Ruth ate him alive," Dave said with a stunning lack of tact. "I'm glad he has you."

Jenny's shoe caught on the pavement, and she stumbled forward. "Oh!"

He caught her hand as it groped outward. Holding it for a moment, he said, "You'll have to forgive me for this. I've always been short. Perhaps that's been part of my trouble. I just want you to know that I understand how Everett feels, partly because I look at you and like what I see, partly because I really love that man."

She swallowed down a knot in her throat. "Dave, Everett and I have known each other . . ." she turned her hand—"since forever. I know him pretty well. I'm glad he has you too. But don't misconstrue . . ."

She found it impossible to say more to this man whom she barely knew.

He covered her hand. "It's okay. I'm not prying. Just . . . if you ever need a friend, and I say this from experience, know that you've got one."

The highway would be opening within the hour, the waiter was informing everyone in the cafe when they returned. Everyone was checking out of the hotel. Traffic would be bad for the major part of the morning, but at least they could get through.

Withdrawing some bills from his wallet, Everett placed them upon the table. His staff, eager to leave before the needle swung over into Everett's danger zone, scraped their chairs to rise.

"Thank God," said Ruth, throwing her blond hair from around her face.

As Ruth walked away, Jenny stood behind Everett's right shoulder. She watched her stop to say something to the cleaning man, who had ceased mopping as she walked across. As she passed, the man watched her for an uncomfortable moment.

Turning, pocketing his wallet as if the whole meal had exhausted him, Everett said, "I'm very sorry about that, Jen. Ruth is the last person I expected."

"Facing our mistakes is never expected." Why had she said that? "Oh, now I'm sorry. If Ruth was a mistake, she was an understandable one."

"I don't want your understanding about Ruth. Jenny—"

"She's obviously brilliant, Everett. And lovely."

Beyond them, Ruth slouched modishly against the registration desk, chatting gaily with the matron.

"Yes, Ruth is very nice. Jenny, look at me."

Jenny refused to turn around. She stood in a stream of soft morning light and zipped and unzipped her handbag. She felt his discomfort in waves.

"Dammit, Jenny," he warned, "don't do this."

"Up until a few minutes ago she wasn't real," Jenny mumbled. "I could hate her and not feel guilty about it."

Everett feared desperately that he was letting Jenny slip through his fingers. "I want you to go home, Jen. Now. Today."

Jenny's face tipped upward, the strain having taken its toll in the lines about her eyes, the slope of her shoulders. "I would've thought you'd want me to stay. Especially now."

"I don't want you hurt."

No anger was on her face when she said, "You can hurt me, Everett. No one else."

"I know I can. God knows, I don't mean to."

Everett thought the brown of Jenny's irises was unfathomable. He read her pain in their small, clear circles. He reached for her hand. She drew back her shoulder.

"Not here." She shook her head. "Not in Spain. Not . . ." She was thinking of his request for her to live with him in Boston. ". . . not the way things are."

She expected him to protest. Down deep inside her she wanted to hear him say that nothing could keep him from loving her, least of all Ruth. But Everett was caught up in watching something himself.

Jenny followed the path of his gaze. A small toddler was fretting in his father's arms to be let down on the floor. When the man bent and placed the boy on his feet, the child, in his wobbly fashion, scooted across the room. His mother laughed back at the man and followed her son, catching him by the collar of his blue Windbreaker.

Glancing back at Everett, Jenny thought she'd never witnessed such naked hunger. Nor such unspeakable weariness when he found her watching him.

"Is that why you don't want to get married?" Jenny asked. "Because you'd be reminded that you're not virile, or whatever garbage men think about themselves in these circumstances?"

Everett let her remark sink in, hating it because it was true. He stumbled ever so slightly.

"Damn, but you've got a vicious streak in you."

She wanted to fling her arms about his neck, to say she was sorry, to beg him to forgive her for putting his private fear into words. But he was looking out over the lobby at the mass of people finishing up business, anxious to leave.

"I'm staying," she said to his shoulder blades. "I started this, and I want to finish it. I really mean that. But I want what happened last night to be what it is—an interlude that can't ever be repeated. If you care anything about me at all, Everett, you'll do it my way."

Please let him say there was no way he could live with an ultimatum like that!

Everett sighed the sigh of a beaten man. "We have a lot of work ahead of us. I'm afraid I can't always be there to watch out for you, Jenny. It's my opinion you should go back home, but since you won't, listen to one who knows. Keep out of Ruth's way."

He turned abruptly and strode to the desk, where the line of departing guests was growing longer.

"I'm sorry," she whispered, but he didn't hear.

Chapter Seven

Ouch!"

Jenny failed to dodge swiftly enough as a bronze-skinned national swung around with a section of vacuum hose. At nine o'clock in the morning he was operating a giant machine that sucked up the residue of mud and debris left by the shovel crews. The hose caught her on the side. She stumbled, dropping her clipboard with a clatter.

In a profusion of agitated Castilian the stocky man apologized. He shook his half-bald head and waved his hands. He hurriedly retrieved her clipboard, gave her a bow that was comically akin to a curtsy, and ended by blowing her a penitent kiss.

"He says he's *mucho, mucho* sorry, señora," laughed Serita, Jenny's dark-eyed assistant, who seconded as translator for Jenny. She was a young woman and still secure enough with her beauty to go without makeup and sleek her hair back in a severe ponytail.

"He would rather have his hands crushed than to hurt one hair of the señora's beautiful head." Serita added the final interpretation.

Jenny pulled a smiling grimace. "Tell him that isn't necessary. If he'll get this side of the building clean enough so we can come in after lunch with the paint crews, I'll . . ."

"No promises." Serita held up her hands, palms out. "They take everything literally."

"Then tell him he didn't hurt me at all." Jenny nursed her ribs by holding her arm to her side. He'd nearly knocked the breath out of her.

Serita, who was on her way with some memos that would coordinate the engineers' repair of the wiring and plumbing to Jenny's treatment of walls and floors, left with her usual ribbing about Jenny's Georgian drawl. "Foreigner," she called back as she waved. "Can't understand a thing you say."

Jenny tucked her clipboard against her good side. After nearly two weeks of battling contaminated water, a foot of mud on every floor, blocked air-conditioner ducts, and ruined wall surfaces, the worst of the cleanup was nearly done. Every morning commenced with an inspection of the half-mile-long building of laboratories and storage rooms. It was a task she enjoyed. Watching things transform brought out some latent sense of power inside her. Today she was about to go over the rooms fronting the north side. The painting, hopefully, could begin tomorrow. The damaged portions of the wall could be covered in a vinyl product, and that could be trimmed out and refurnished. This place was better because she'd been here, she thought with self-satisfying pride.

She bunched the legs of burgundy wool slacks into the tops of heavy rubber boots. What a picture she must present. She had removed her blazer and put on a long smock. It was yards too big and drooped past her knees. She looked like a Munchkin from Oz. Oh, well, she mused as she began compiling her report, no one cared what anyone else looked like, not after tromping around in this muck all day.

Ruth, though not actively involved in the process of restoration, nonetheless made her presence felt as a member of the board. She could be seen at almost any time talking to the men, supervising, giving instructions. Jenny had to respect the woman's expertise. She wouldn't have expected Everett to marry an imbecile. And she went far out of her way to behave in a modern, "civilized" way to Everett's ex-wife.

"Great outfit," Ruth called now as she spied Jenny in one of the hallways. She gestured from Jenny's head to her feet. "A Paris creation?"

Jenny viewed Ruth's open smock coat and four-hundred-dollar slacks and jacket beneath it.

"Panama Canal," she answered with a studied lack of intimacy. "Cost me a fortune."

Ruth laughed. "You know, I think we're getting this thing under control. Thank heaven the offices don't require too much. If they hadn't been built on that higher slope, we'd have all that to do too."

"A small blessing."

"But the insurance settlement will be terrible. It's a flood, of course, but one caused by vandalism. Everett's conducting a small war with the insurance people today."

"Is that so?"

"Everett conducts wonderful wars. He fights dirty."

From the moment she and Everett had landed on the perimeter of the ocean of mud, Jenny had seen more of Ruth than him. When she did catch a glimpse, he was usually walking through the debris, accompanied by dark-suited men wearing knee-high boots and exceedingly grim looks. If he wasn't raising additional money, he was on the telephone, his tie askew, with a line of people fretting to see him. For the most part the communication between them had consisted of weighty looks telegraphed across a maze of activity. At the end of the first week she found a memo tacked on the door of her motor home: *You're saving my life*, it read. *I think of you constantly*.

Now she and Ruth veered into one of the gutted laboratories. The empty walls echoed the clatter of Ruth's heels like the sound track of a movie. Immediately Jenny moved to an outside wall and studied a crack that branched from the floor halfway to the ceiling. Since yesterday it had grown several inches, which indicated internal damage to the footings.

"I told Serita to have one of the engineers take a look at this," she told Ruth, giving the crack a pat.

Ruth flicked her lighter and blew smoke as she bent nearer the wall. "You're right. The footings have probably shifted."

"Does the center of the wall seem to sag to you?" Jenny took several steps back and surveyed the entire wall like an artist pondering a canvas.

Ruth narrowed her eyes. She callously flicked ashes where the cleaning men had just vacuumed. "Since you mention it, yes. I'll make sure Serita gets Josh on this. He's good at this sort of troubleshooting."

Except for the crack, there remained no more work in this particular group of labs. Expecting Ruth to leave, too, Jenny moved toward the door.

The blond woman lagged behind. "I've been watching you work, Jennifer. You're quite good at what you do."

The compliment put Jenny on guard. "Thank you."

"You and Everett have known each other for years, he tells me. Yet, he never mentioned you to me. I find that strange, don't you?"

"Men never tell everything."

"You're wrong. It's the women who never tell."

"Perhaps."

Hoping this conversation would go no further, Jenny bent over a box of assorted cables and switches. She picked up a toggle switch and absently flipped it. If Ruth didn't hold the position she did, she would say she had work to do and walk out.

Ruth took a long drag of her cigarette. "I want him back."

At first Jenny thought Ruth was making some razor-edged joke. But she wasn't. Her green eyes were clear and merciless and truthful. Jenny didn't know what to do. Pretending to misunderstand the repercussions of such a statement would have been ridiculous.

She dropped the switch back into the box as if a live current had sparked through it, burning her.

"You're surprised?"

Jenny let the lie find the tip of her tongue. "It's no concern of mine."

"It's very much your concern. You're in love with him."

Someone was inside her head, beating upon her eardrums with a steel mallet. "*Love* is a vague term," Jenny heard herself saying in a shockingly normal voice. "Highly overused."

"There's nothing vague about the term *affair*. Are you having an affair with my ex-husband, Jennifer?"

Time missed a beat. Jenny saw herself sitting in her tree house in the willow tree. She felt the heat of the Georgia summers and grew slowly aware of the present chill in the room, as if the life-giving blood in her veins had ceased to flow. She spun briskly on her heel.

"I didn't judge you a woman who would do that."

"Do what?" Jenny asked stupidly from the doorway. She didn't remember walking there.

"You looked like a fighter to me."

"Fools stay to fight bears. I've never considered myself to be a fool." Nausea swam up in her throat.

"Of course not. You're a very bright girl, Jennifer. And pretty. All of Everett's mistresses were bright and pretty. I didn't wish anything bad for them, and I don't wish anything bad for you. I just don't want you to have Everett."

"What Everett does with his own life—"

"I made a mistake in divorcing Everett," Ruth said. "It was all my fault. Oh, he might tell you otherwise, but it was."

There was no counterfeit friendliness about Ruth now, only a stony coldness like emerald. "Go home, Jennifer Howard. Forget Everett. You'll only get hurt."

Reckless anger now replaced any despair Jenny had felt. Her hands started trembling uncontrollably. The taste of cotton filled her mouth and her voice cracked as she took one step toward the other woman.

"I don't think you know exactly how Everett feels about you . . ." Jenny began.

"It doesn't matter how he feels." Ruth smiled. "I have an ultimate weapon, and I don't mind using it."

Was this what Everett had warned her about? Ruth's remarkable ability to hurt? She'd had enough of this. She turned. "I consider myself warned."

"I'm going to get pregnant."

It took some seconds for the words to register for what they were. At first Jenny's logic refused to consider them as being credible. Ruth was just threatening, wasn't she, as when a person said "I could kill you" but didn't mean it at all?

"He always wanted a child with me," she heard Ruth

saying to her back. "Now do you understand what I mean when I say go home and forget him?"

Before Jenny realized it, she was ruinously exposed. She stood stripped of all her protective devices. She remembered feeling the same way during the worst throes of childbirth—totally at someone else's mercy.

She grasped for the most primitive of all self-protections. "Be my guest!" she cried defiantly, spinning around. "Have a dozen children!"

Jenny didn't wait for Ruth's reaction. She darted from the room and moved quickly through the work crews to a bathroom that was functioning. The tears were already brimming, spilling. She bumped into faceless men and was steadied by anonymous hands. Now she knew what Everett had meant. What cruel indifference Ruth was capable of! What brutality!

She slammed the door to the mud-coated room and giddily flipped the lock. Leaning her head upon the wall, not caring that it was caked with dried crust from many hands, she wept until she could hardly stand up. She closed the toilet seat and lowered herself to sit. She blew her nose several times and waited for the nauseous spasms to leave her stomach.

Pregnant? No woman could truly love a man if she would stoop to a trick like that. Besides, Ruth couldn't get pregnant. *Or could she?*

The truth—utterly unexpected, utterly bizarre—came with the force of a karate chop at the base of Jenny's skull. Ruth was planning on getting pregnant. *Ruth* was the reason Everett had never become a father. And he'd lived years thinking there was something wrong with him.

A pain knifed up the back of her head, and Jenny clapped a hand to her neck. Poor Everett. Poor, darling Everett.

Rising, blinking at her splotchy reflection in the mirror, Jenny began splashing cold water on her face. She slowly stopped. She looked at her hands, her wet, ringless hands, and then back to her red-eyed self. Her jaw dropped in horror and she drew in a breath of air.

"Oh, you fool," she whispered. "You stupid little fool. You're the one who'll end up pregnant."

Her hands automatically reached for her belly. There was no way she could have been in a safe time in her month. No way at all. They had made love all night. And the last thing he'd said was he wouldn't get her pregnant! *Oh, Everett, what have we done?*

She walked out of the room in a daze. Feeling lost, as if she were a child who had awakened in a strange bed and couldn't find a familiar object, she scanned the distance between the complex and the office buildings. Then she remembered Everett was meeting with the insurance men. She had to talk to him. She would find him tonight at his room in the office building. She didn't care how many eyebrows she raised.

Ruth Black breezed through the complex later that day with the self-assurance of one highly skilled at the art of instigating trouble. At college the other girls had called her a bitch because of the time bombs she planted. But she loved the way she felt when she "entered the fray." Her adrenaline surged; vitality charged through her. She felt wonderful. And she knew she looked wonderful. Heads turned as she swept by. And the men, seeming to sense that she thrived on it, muttered obscenities loud enough for her to hear. One whistled under his breath. She tossed him a demure smile.

Spotting Serita near the engineers' headquarters in a temporary aluminum building, Ruth called out.

Turning, Serita shaded her eyes. "What's up?" the younger woman said, smiling.

"Nothing except a few sexual appetites. Men are such stupid creatures, aren't they?"

Serita knew better than to reply to that one.

"Are you on your way to the engineers' building?" Ruth laughed. It was well known that Serita had a thing for the abrasive Josh McClellan.

Serita toyed with the buttons on her jacket. "I was just coming back. I told Josh about that crack on the north wall. Mrs. Howard asked me to."

Patting for her cigarettes, Ruth casually asked, "What crack?"

"The one that's going to ruin the whole side if the footing isn't fixed."

"Really?" Ruth's lighter flared. A group of men walked past, and she watched them with heavy-lidded eyes. "I was just talking to Jennifer about that crack. She's decided it's probably a temperature change. A patch job will be enough."

"Patch job!"

Ruth shrugged and continued watching the men. She smiled when one threw her a backward glance. "Well, she is supposed to be an expert about those things, you know. Everett brought her specifically for it. Go back and tell Josh to forget it."

"But, Mrs. Black . . ."

"Tell him to forget it. And round up someone to get the thing patched so we can get the paint crew started immediately."

Letting her shoulders drop, for she'd been looking forward to following Josh over to the complex and spending some time with him, Serita grudgingly obeyed. She shook her head as she went. She wasn't

sure if she trusted Jennifer Howard's judgment anymore.

"What addle-brained jerk did this?" roared Josh
McClellan. He towered before the north wall, his thick,
meaty hands braced upon his hips, his baseball cap
turned backward on his head. A cigar rolled untidily
between his teeth. He removed it and jabbed it at Ruth
Black. "Did you do this?"

The three of them—Ruth, Serita, and Josh—were in
the center of a loosely formed circle of national labor-
ers. The crack in the wall was drying nicely, and the
paint crew had already begun redoing the ceiling. Spray
guns were set up and cans of paint and rollers cluttered
the floor. Light fixtures and switch plates had all been
removed.

Ruth smiled innocently. "I knew the order to patch it
had gone through, yes. But I thought—"

"Did you order it?"

"Well, no. Mrs. Howard did, as a matter of fact. But
I talked with her about it. It seemed to me to be a clear
matter of the footings having shifted, Josh, what with
the wall drooping that way. But she said . . ."

Josh muttered a vile word that made the two women
exchange a grimace. They wisely remained silent. "Get
her, Serita. Get this paragon in here. Sweet mercy,
can't I trust a woman to do anything without fouling it
up?"

As Serita met Ruth's pleased smile with dumbfounded confusion, Ruth shook her head very slightly. "Do
as the man says, honey. It's out of our hands now."

Jenny was popping the top from a canned soft drink
when Serita found her and delivered the message.
Sipping, she dropped the piece of aluminum in a
trash can and blotted her mouth on the back of her
hand.

"Josh McClellan wants to see me?" she inquired. She hoped there was a mistake. She wasn't particularly fond of the bristly, sometimes crude civil engineer. "I thought it was up to him to examine the footings. Surely he doesn't need my opinion about that."

A pained expression passed over Serita's face. She was a simply raised Castilian brought up in a devoutly religious family. Her dark eyes welled at being trapped in this position. She shrugged as if she couldn't imagine why Josh would do such a thing.

Jenny sipped again and relished the sharp sting of the carbonated water. "Well, perhaps the stars have lined up right, Serita. Maybe the old porcupine only wants to admit women have been invented."

"Mrs. Howard—"

Frowning as the vibes warned her like the yellowing of the sky before a high wind, Jenny paused in the congested walkway. "What's the matter, Serita? Something's wrong. Tell me."

The Spanish girl smoothed back a lock of black hair. She couldn't risk her future on something that wasn't any of her business. "I don't know anything, Mrs. Howard. Honest."

Jenny had lived with her temperamental Jeffrey too long to accept a pat answer like that. She gingerly strode toward the north laboratories. What a rotten day this had turned out to be: Ruth telling her that she'd tricked Everett all their married life and now Josh McClellan. She'd be glad to see the last of Spain, money or no money.

The moment Jenny stepped into the room where she and Ruth had had their earlier confrontation, her fingers tightened about the soft drink can. Dark liquid spilled. Keeping her eyes glued to the apprehension straining the faces of the nationals, she absently licked her fingers.

"Ah, she arrives," came Josh's deep sarcasm. "Like the new Prince of Wales. We've been waiting, Mrs. Howard."

With his feet widespread, standing directly in front of her as if he were going to start a fistfight, he removed the baseball cap. He ran his fingers through his hair and settled it back on his head.

"Well"—she made herself smile as she would smile to Alan Kendall—"it's nice to be classed in such high regard as the Prince of Wales. Is there some difficulty?"

"Difficulty?" he thundered. "Do you consider the collapse of this end of the building a difficulty? Or doesn't it matter to you that two million dollars' worth of building could come to nothing during the first winter freeze?" McClellan threw out a hand toward the drying wall.

The ominous crack was now a well-mended seam of gray plaster, a craggy design upon some psychiatrist's test: What word does this bring to mind? the doctor would have asked. Lightning, she would have replied. The splintering disaster of lightning.

She maintained her be-polite-to-the-difficult-client voice. "Oh, it's been repaired," she said pleasantly, though she suffered a wave of confusion. "I see—"

"Of course it's been repaired. Like the road to hell after all your good intentions, Mrs. Howard."

The lightning was flashing about her head now, warning her of the storm, but she didn't know where to duck for shelter.

"There's no need to be rude, Mr. McClellan. I only meant that I'm surprised the crack is being repaired at all. It was my understanding—"

"Then you did look at it and send word to me."

Didn't the man believe in finishing sentences? "Yes, I looked at it."

"Then I don't see how you hold a job, Mrs. Howard. In fact, when Black gets in this evening, I'm going to recommend that he replace you."

"Now wait a minute."

"Minute? I'd say that's about all the time you gave this wall."

McClellan's mockery was making the room so uncomfortable, the onlookers began to shift and squirm. Jenny's baffled look met that of Ruth. The blonde stood with her arms folded over her bosom. She seemed to be enjoying the sight of the man's temper. She smiled at Jenny.

"Can't you see the sagging, my dear?" The condescension grew syrupy in his voice. "The footings have deteriorated. Any idiot could tell that. Yet, you think several thousand dollars' worth of remodeling like a Band-Aid could hold it. My, you women really like to go on spending sprees."

Now Jenny understood, at least partially, the strange distress on Serita's face and the gloating smile on Ruth's. Somewhere her recommendations to Josh McClellan had been distorted. Whether intentionally or not was hardly worth considering.

An old familiar rage at injustice raced through Jenny's veins. She felt nerves popping in the backs of her legs and tried to keep enough of a perspective to stop this before it progressed any further.

"I don't think this is the time or place to resolve this," she said, and threw out her hand at the people standing around. "These men need to get to work."

"Too bad you didn't think of economy when you sent word saying you'd changed your mind, missy."

Jenny stepped up to the towering man—David about to attack Goliath with his bare hands.

"For an educated man, Mr. McClellan," she said through her teeth, "you're sadistically intolerant. In my business we put facts together before we jump to conclusions!"

The clear gray eyes of the engineer widened in amazement. "Are you one of those hell-raising liberators who thinks everybody's out to gun 'em down?" he yelled.

"No! I'm one of those hell raisers who says a person has a right to be heard before all the evidence is in. Did Serita tell you I'd decided to call in an expert from Barcelona?"

Josh made a ceremony of removing his cigar and flicking the ash. He clamped it between his teeth before he took the clever hook she'd baited.

"No," he said. "She told me you'd decided not to have me look at the wall. If I hadn't done it on my own, we'd have been sued."

Poor Serita's face was hardly to be described when Jenny shook her head in a sad look of *How could you?* She was an insignificant casualty in a war she didn't even understand the rules to. Bright tears were sliding over the black curtain of her lashes. She muttered something in Castilian.

Josh McClellan bellowed at her to speak English.

"I'm sorry," she wept.

"What do you mean, you're sorry? Did the woman say to patch it or not?"

"I only do what I'm told."

Josh paled slightly. He uneasily began rebuckling his belt to his safari jacket.

Turning to the workmen, Jenny told them in broken Spanish to begin gathering up their equipment. They blinked back at her with sullen eyes, but they did as they were ordered.

"And who gave you your orders, young lady?" raged the engineer at the distraught girl. "If it's not too much to ask."

"Mrs. Black."

Josh looked as if he'd taken a blow to the stomach. In one respect he and Serita shared a common bond; he didn't relish the thoughts of jeopardizing his job in a confrontation with a member of the board. He took one look at Ruth's slightly amused face and threw down his cigar in grand disgust.

"Well, I'll be damned," he muttered. "When you ladies get this mess worked out between yourselves, send somebody to tell me. 'Course I don't expect you to go out of your way or anything like that." He began walking out of the room, muttering, "Nothing but a passel of eye-scratchin' cats. I'll swear to God. . . ."

Serita gave a groan of humiliated defeat and walked like an aging woman from the room.

Positioning herself before the windows, Jenny kept her back to the crew as they finished emptying the room of equipment to be cleaned. She needed the time to compose herself before she walked through the building and across the complex. It had all grown too big, hadn't it—her need for Everett, the differences in what they wanted, this unexpected treachery from Ruth? Things had been so simple when she had lived only for her children and kept the lonely vigil of the nights to herself.

Something for which she had no name—an anxious, crawling sensation—presently made her hug herself. She'd be glad to get out of here.

Ruth was leaning against the opposite wall when she turned, watching her. Jenny's surprise paralyzed her tongue.

Everett's ex-wife walked to the same group of windows but kept to the far end, as if Jenny were contagious. Neither said a word. They looked out at chunks of the sidewalk washed out of the ground like so many square soda crackers.

After a time Ruth said quietly, "You didn't think I'd let you leave without making sure, did you?"

This woman had beaten her, Jenny thought numbly. She should have known from that moment in the little hotel in Talencia that Ruth would win. "I suppose that was naive thinking."

"You didn't believe me, Jennifer," Ruth explained, as if it were a legitimate reason and Jenny should accept it. "I could tell you didn't take me seriously. I did what I did—with McClellan—to make you know I mean to win. There was nothing really personal in it."

Jenny looked at her with a total lack of comprehension for the way her mind worked. "My mother is a religious woman," she said tonelessly, and began walking away. "She always used to quote a Scripture to me. Your mother should have taught it to you."

"Look, Jennifer—"

Reaching the doorway now, something she hadn't been positive she could do, Jenny said, "A very old principle, actually. 'Be sure, your sin will find you out.' It always does, Ruth. Count on it."

"What sin?" demanded Everett as Jenny backed into him.

Chapter Eight

"What sin?"

Everett's voice rumbled from just behind Jenny's head as he repeated his demand, a distant thunder emanating from a bank of approaching storm clouds. His hands closed upon her arms to prevent her from tripping backward upon his feet.

Regaining her balance, brushing his hands away, Jenny swiveled about. How much had he heard?

He was tired; she could see that much. His eyes, bloodshot and tense, seemed burdened with his own corruptible humanity. Yet, his control—the one perpetual thing she could depend on—was intact, as inflexible as the deep lines framing his mouth. Everett Black was in no mood for games.

"What are you doing here?" Not until the words were out did she realize how stupid they sounded.

Everett twisted at the knot of his tie and worked it free. Grimacing against his shirt collar, he unbuttoned it. Standing there with it draped about his neck, he held each end of it.

"I work here," he said with colorless irony. He let his perusal flick skeptically from her to his ex-wife.

Ruth slouched modishly near the window, lighting a cigarette.

"What are you doing, Jenny?" he said, almost as if he didn't expect an answer, continuing to drill into Ruth. "Besides sending my head engineer into orbit?"

"Josh?"

"He chewed his cigar to shreds and was threatening to quit when I left him at the helicopter pad. My suspicions were beginning to be aroused by then." He still didn't look at Jenny.

The moment was infuriating. Jenny cursed the situation she suddenly found herself in. If she defended her position over the repairs, Ruth would only shoot her down. If she didn't, Everett had no choice but to accept the word of his engineer and an active member of the board that she was a klutz. Either way she came out looking like a fool.

She swung around to face Ruth's smirk without any pretense of politeness.

A sly smile turned up the corners of the other woman's mouth. Her green eyes glinted with the hardness of a cat's when its back was arched to fight. *I warned you, didn't I?* her plucked brows reminded.

Conceding Ruth the victory and not caring, at this point, that she'd lost, Jenny said tightly, "What I'm doing, Everett, is leaving this room."

"Like hell you are."

Everett broke his tenacious inspection of his ex-wife. He attached his back to the doorjamb and crossed his ankles as though time were his greatest luxury. He motioned Jenny back into the room with a smile she thoroughly mistrusted.

Ruth stirred. Her heels intruded into the quiet. "There's been trouble here today, Everett." She raised her voice superciliously. Anyone in the hall could have heard her.

He sighed. "Isn't there always?"

"Take care of it."

"Did it ever occur to you, Ruth, that a person could get weary of cleaning up your messes?"

Without relinquishing her officious stance, Ruth jerked her face up and away. It was an affected gesture, as if he had slapped her and she had accepted it with a patience that had suffered long and grievously.

I shouldn't be a party to this, Jenny told herself. This was between the two of them. She should be on the other side of the world.

"And you'd better waste no time doing it," Ruth's red-nailed fingers flicked toward Jenny, "before things get out of hand."

Openmouthed, Jenny watched Everett transform without warning. She had once wondered if anything could break through that veneer of composure. Now, when it did, she was dumbfounded. His right hand slammed against the wall in a backhanded blow so vicious he had to have felt the shock clear to his skull. Rage blazed in his eyes and his color was ghastly.

Everett nearly lifted Ruth from the floor when his hands crushed her shoulders.

The haughtiness drained from Ruth's face. She trembled with a desperate need to calm him. "Everett! My, God, get ahold of yourself!"

"You've gone too far this time, Ruth." Everett's razor-edged fury slashed through the empty room. "You've hurt something I care about."

Ruth shuddered, frightened. "You're hurting me!"

He gritted through his teeth. "If you dare touch her again, Ruth . . ." He lifted one hand.

"Everett!" cried Jenny, flying to his side, fearing that he would actually strike the woman. She caught his arm and pulled hard, fighting him in her soundless way as strenuously as he was fighting Ruth.

Not only was Jenny certain that Everett had never been driven to this point before, she doubted that he'd ever even yelled at Ruth. The woman was horrified and shivering. Jenny envisioned quiet, terrible cruelties occurring in their marriage, and she clung to Everett, willing him to let Ruth go.

Everett was spent. He felt as if the life had drained out of him when he learned about Jenny's ordeal, something he should have had the sense to foresee. He looked at Jenny's stricken face and, paling slightly, released Ruth.

"You deserve everything that happens to you," he told Ruth with a gravity that was more terrifying than his passion.

Ruth's face wasn't that of a beautiful woman any longer. Her hatred of Everett, clearly visible now, clawed ravaged lines down her face. And her panic had turned her gray and haggard. Up until that moment Jenny had hated her for what she'd done to Everett, cheating him of his paternity. Now, thinking that this alien, empty room was symbolic of what Ruth had to look forward to for the rest of her life, she felt nothing but pity.

The moment Everett released her, Ruth whirled away to put some space between them. "You can't treat me like this and get by with it. I'm a stockholding member of this board, Everett!" She looked at Jenny as if it were imperative that she understand her power. "I *am* a stockholding member of the board, you know." Then, to Everett: "I will make things very unpleasant for you. Don't think I won't."

Everett walked to the window and gave both women

his back. He took a few moments to steady himself and adjusted his shoulders back into his jacket. He regretted losing control. He sighed heavily, bitterly.

"I cut my teeth on your unpleasantries, Ruth. If you don't agree with my policies, why don't you resign the board?"

"Drop dead."

"I've offered to buy out your stock."

"I'm not interested in selling."

His voice was unbelievably cold when he spun on his heel. He was visibly holding onto the shreds of his tolerance. "Sell!"

The silence, when it finally came, was deathlike in its intensity. Though Jenny was ignorant of the full implications of their battle, she knew that neither of them were. They knew exactly what they were doing and why.

With her pretenses finally stripped away, Ruth strode swiftly to the door. She paused a moment to send Jenny a look that would have drawn blood had it been physical. Smiling then, as if she had no doubts, she placed the fingers of one hand behind her neck. Her chin lifted.

"I come very high, Everett." She shook her hair back from her face and pronounced each word with weight. "I don't think you can afford to buy me."

"That isn't the point," Everett replied with a valiant recovery of his demeanor. He shifted his weight to one hip and masked his anger as perfectly as if it had never erupted. "The point is, can Rich Mansfield afford you?"

The green of Ruth's eyes flashed. Her mouth curled in stunned outrage, and disgust pinched her nostrils.

Everett shrugged. "And will Rich even want to if . . ."

The red slash of Ruth's lips looked like a terrible wound. "You wouldn't dare."

"My dear, I leave that up to you," he said.

Ruth began shaking. "At least Rich is a contemporary thinker, Everett Black. He isn't buried in the Dark Ages anymore. He isn't walking around in a righteous funk, sermonizing about the friends I have."

"Paramours aren't friends, Ruth," Everett intoned wearily.

Aiming a finger at him, Ruth threw back her head in a magnificent performance. "You bastard!" she hissed. As she swept out the door, she yelled at Jenny, "He wasn't this way before you came along!"

The room was very still after she left. Jenny and Everett met the eyes of the other in mute distaste of what had happened. Keeping the wide expanse between them, Jenny inched back against the wall. Exhausted, she leaned against it and slid down until she was sitting.

Everett unbuttoned his vest with a sad exhaustion. He studied her limp form and dropped to his knees before the windows. The building was emptying. The quietness of it was settling like the calmness of slumber after a fever.

"I'm sorry," he said, and braced his elbows upon his knees. He let his head sink into his hands. "Now you know."

Jenny wasn't sure she could even speak. "And what do I know?"

"How bad it can get." His voice was muffled behind his hands. "Why I'm afraid to lay myself on the line again. To take a chance again."

She wondered if he could have looked at her and said it. She wanted, in the depths of her empathy, to hold him. "I knew that before, Everett."

Everett reached beyond his limit for something to cauterize the gaping injury between them. He straightened his knees and let his hands drop to his lap. He pressed his palms to his waist. "Bear with me, Jenny," he said so quietly she hardly heard the words. "Don't stop loving me."

She'd never said those words to him. For days she'd watched this man at his work, the way he drove himself for something he believed the world needed. How did he know? When had he looked inside her heart and seen what was there?

Slowly, for the day had been cruel, she rose to her feet. Thinking he needed to be alone, she said, "I'll see you later. I have to go now."

She left him with the shattered wreckage of his marriage.

Jenny hurried down the hall, anxious to clear her head of a pounding that seemed intolerable. She was glad the two weeks were up, she told herself. Ruth had been mercilessly honest about her intentions of getting Everett back, but at least Jenny knew where she stood on that score. She loved Everett, yes, but she wearied of this triangle that shouldn't even exist. She felt drained because she loved a man who separated his trust from his love. She missed her children. She needed the support of her mother. She wanted to go home.

It didn't occur to Jenny that Everett would follow her out of the building. Clipped masculine steps rang behind her as she rushed. She pretended not to hear them. She pretended not to care that people were averting their eyes and lifting their brows in commentary about the boss striding several paces behind the young woman from America. She hurried faster.

"If you don't wait for me, Jenny," Everett ground

out to her back, "you're going to think this afternoon's trouble was a party." His voice was deadly serious.

Tight-lipped and impassive, she stopped and waited for him. She had no intentions, however, of telling him anything she and Ruth had talked about.

Everett wearily touched her elbow. "And don't look at me with those Bambi eyes, either. We're going to talk if it takes all night and ruins both our reputations in the process."

"I'm already ahead of you on the reputation," she replied with pretended self-effacement. "I've been working on it all day. Ask Josh."

Looking at her—her tousled curly head topping a smock that was comically too big, her seriousness not fitting the scene, and the independent angle of her chin that was totally unsuitable—Everett couldn't help but grin.

"Sweetheart," he shook his head, "you've been ahead of me all my life."

When she impishly pouted, he chuckled. "And I'm not surprised about your reputation. Not with that . . ." He swept his fingers downward. "What *is* that you're wearing? You look like an expectant Raggedy Ann doll."

Jenny had forgotten what she looked like. She glanced down at herself, and the sides of her mouth curled downward.

Without uttering a word, she unbuttoned the smock, draped it on a hanger she fetched from a rack where everyone hung their coats, and retrieved her own jacket. Everett held it while she slipped into it. He pulled it securely onto her shoulders and stood for some seconds without removing his hands.

"There's something I've been wanting to tell you for days," he said solemnly.

Jenny made a great effort to be logical, but the husky poignancy in his words made it impossible. She could hear his quick, hard breaths. She could almost feel the blood racing through him.

She turned, hoping to see his heart brimming in his eyes. "Tell me what?"

"That . . ." He caught the edge of his upper lip between his teeth, as if weighing things in his mind.

"Later," he promised, and took her hand.

The late afternoon had brought wind with it, and colder weather than they'd had up until now. An overcast sky was painting a film of haze in the air. Green pines and cork oaks seemed cheerless as they bent and accepted their punishment with a muted whine. It all made the chaotic mass of hills that marked the path of the river appear more lonely than ever, as if it regretted that destruction had raced through its screes.

"So, Jennifer Howard," Everett sounded less strained as they dodged the worst of the mud and deepest ruts on the way to her motor home, "if you don't mind, would you please tell me, in your own inimitable fashion, what happened between you and Ruth this afternoon?"

Pain rolled out before Jenny like a road with no place to turn around. She hated lying to him, but what choice did she have? There had to be times when a lie was more the truth than the truth. How could she say to him, *Everett, you're not sterile, you're only a fool.* Better for him to believe a lie than to be crushed by a truth as heartbreaking as Ruth's.

"You know her," she replied, and kept her eyes on her boots. "You saw. You heard."

Everett's reply was muttered so softly she almost didn't hear it.

She blinked at him in amazement. "I didn't know anyone actually said that word."

He stopped walking. "That's nothing compared to what I'm going to say to you if you don't stop playing games with me. I know the truth. Serita told me."

Not all the truth, she thought unhappily. "Then why're you badgering me?"

He pushed her glasses up from where they'd slid down the bridge of her nose. "Because it fills some sadistic quirk in my character," he retorted, then grew swiftly stern. "Because I don't know *why* it happened, dammit!"

Feeling her own eyes snapping, thinking he wouldn't be so flippant if he'd been on the receiving end of Ruth's warped mind, then realizing he'd been on the receiving end for years, she tromped through the mud.

"Try to think in terms of when and where, Everett," she called over her shoulder. "It's much more satisfying."

Praying he wouldn't press the matter further if she simply dismissed it, Jenny strode toward the campsite skirting what had once been the lawn. For nearly two weeks this had been her home.

The campers and motor homes that had been brought in for the crews clustered in a circular group about two hundred yards from the lab building. They resembled, Jenny had thought a number of times, covered wagons in a shoot-'em-up Western movie.

Jenny wobbily made her way across her boarded walk and, boots squishing, stood on tiptoe to reach for the door of her vehicle. From behind her Everett brushed her hand aside and pulled the door open. Her instincts, when she saw the familiar determination on his face, were to clamber up the steps and slam the door.

Everett didn't comment after he'd handed her up. He hefted himself into the tiny vehicle and overpowered the entrance with his body. A chill breezed through the room. With one fist stuffed deep in his pockets, his good shoes crusting with mud, he appeared prepared to stand there half the night, looking at her.

"You might as well shut the door," she said without enthusiasm. She balanced herself on one foot as she wrestled with her boot. "You'll freeze us to death."

"At least your Southern hospitality hasn't disappeared with your prudence," he said wryly, and shut the door.

Without asking her, he pushed her down into the seat opposite the driver's and took the other himself. He spread his legs and motioned for her to put her foot on the floor between them. He gave the boot a tug. It came free in his hands.

Looking at it for a moment, as if he would like to say something, he carefully placed it on a piece of newspaper spread for that express purpose. He removed her other boot.

After giving a rueful look at the condition of his own shoes, he bent, slipped one off, then the other. He tossed his suit coat across the driver's seat and stripped the tie from about his neck. It coiled artlessly over the dashboard. Rolling up the sleeves of his shirt, he turned to find her quizzically observing him.

"Oh, there's no cause for alarm," he said with a deprecating grimace. "I'm not taking off any more than that."

When she jerked her head away, he chuckled. "Unless, of course, you'd like me to. I've never been one to tell a lady no."

His joking caught Jenny totally off guard. She took one look at his guileless, handsome face, knowing the enormous tragedy that he didn't even realize he'd been subjected to, and burst into tears. Before he could even express his dismay, she jumped up from her seat and stumbled blindly toward the cubicle that was the bathroom. Was that all she could do today—cry?

She leaned back against the closed door and tried unsuccessfully to quench the hot river of tears. But they refused to stop. The door at her back was shoved open so forcibly that she was driven forward against the sink.

"What the hell is going on, Jenny?" he demanded. "I mean to get to the bottom of this if it's the last thing I do."

Squeezing into the compartment, a procedure that molded him tightly against her hips until the door swung shut, Everett watched her drooping reflection in the mirror.

"Don't look at me." Though it was dark in the small room, for she hadn't turned on any lights, she remained as far from him as possible. "Isn't it enough to have everyone mad at me? Go away, Everett."

"Don't play Camille, Jenny."

"I'm not playing anybody. Go away."

He was helpless to console her. He wanted to hold her. He wanted to be held, but with her in her present mood he didn't dare.

"I'm the boss," he teased halfheartedly. "You can't tell me to go away."

"I'm terminating my employment. As of now."

"Unacceptable."

At least the argument, as foolish as it was, was something they could do together. Everett ripped off some tissue and offered it to her.

She didn't respond.

He forced up her head and held it still while he blotted at her reddened eyes. He pinched her nose lightly. "Blow."

She blew, then gave a half-giggle, half-cry. She

dragged off her glasses with considerable disregard for their fragility and took the tissue from him. With an utter lack of dignity, she lustily blew again.

"You can't quit without giving notice," he teased.

"Take McClellan's recommendation, then. Fire me, because I'm leaving."

"Screw McClellan's recommendation. I do my own hiring and firing. You have two more days, I believe. Which reminds me . . ."

Blotting her tear-laden eyes, Jenny watched Everett graze his fingers over the pocket of his shirt. He paused, smoothing the starched surface, and seemed to ponder.

"Oh, no," he said. "Damn."

"What?" She was compelled to flatten herself against the sink as he opened the door again. Snatching a fresh handful of tissue, she followed him in her stockinged feet as he strode through the tiny vehicle.

He began meticulously going through each pocket of the coat to his suit, then each pocket of his pants.

"What are you looking for?" she finally demanded.

"I've lost them."

"Lost what? Was it important?"

"Of course it was important. Now wait just a minute, I remember putting . . ."

Jenny supressed an exasperated sigh. "If you'd just tell me, Everett, perhaps I could—"

He rubbed his forehead with the tips of his fingers. "I would have sworn I . . ."

Even though she let her eyes close, she was unable to ignore his diligent searching for long. She moved behind his shoulder and placed her hand on his arm. "Now you've got me worried. Maybe I could help. Something about the flood, maybe? Some notes you made?"

He seemed not to hear. He only rummaged through his wallet, removing everything and flipping through it until she thought she would scream.

"Will you tell me what it is?" she cried at last, stepping into him from the front, grabbing his wallet to stop his futile looking.

Swiftly, for she thought him too preoccupied, Everett caught her with an arm about his waist. He pulled her into him until they were touching everywhere from the waist down. Grabbing a handful of her curls with one hand, he gently pulled her head back and gazed down at the helpless white arch of her throat. He moved against her slowly, exquisitely, and moistened his lips.

"These," he said, smiling with a satisfaction that made Jenny positive he'd never lost anything in the first place. He waved two pieces of paper beneath her nose.

With her hand that wasn't clutching his wallet, she grabbed his waving hand. She squinted at what she now saw were two tickets and drew them nearer.

"Will you be still?" Maddened, she squinted to read without her glasses.

He laughed down at her absorption and knew he'd succeeded in taking her mind off Ruth. He released her and gave her a quick slap on her behind. "You blind little bat. They're opera tickets. One of the insurance men gave them to me."

A squeak of excitement bubbled out of her. "Opera? Here?"

"In Barcelona, goose."

Her face fell. "Tonight?"

"Yes, at the Gran Teatro Liceo. I've arranged for a helicopter to take us in and a car at the airport. If you can do something to repair those horrendous red eyes, get dressed."

"This is a joke, isn't it?"

He shook his head. "I'm going to wine you and dine you."

"Poetry and flowers?"

"Only if I have to. Then"—he paused, chuckling—"you owe me."

She didn't know how much was teasing and how much was real. "Alan Kendall says I'm a bad credit risk," she reminded briskly.

Everett had slipped on his jacket, and she absently folded down the back of his collar and brushed off the shoulders, a wifely gesture that was automatic.

"Have no fear. Collecting is my strong point." He glanced up from tying his shoelaces. The teasing glint was missing. "I mean to have my talk."

Watching his hands, his moves, his grace of straightening, Jenny felt an impulse to hold nothing back from him. He was reaching for her through the disorder of his life. She couldn't be imagining it. Shouldn't she tell him the truth about Ruth now? She suddenly caught his hands and lifted them to her lips.

Deeply touched, Everett smiled tenderly down at her. "What did I do to merit that, pretty lady?"

"In a country where everyone else would go to a bullfight, Everett, you're taking me to the opera. What do I do with a man like you?"

He grinned and thought, when her dimples twinkled on each side of her smile, that the three-figure sum it had cost him to arrange this evening was already worth it. How precious she was to him.

"I don't suppose you'd know what they're performing, would you?" she inquired sweetly, looping his tie and drawing the end through to fashion a perfectly dreadful knot.

He drew himself up as if she'd just made him one of

the ten best-dressed men of the world. *"Carmen,"* he said. "What else?"

By the time that Everett grabbed Jenny's hand and darted with her beneath the backwash of the helicopter propellers, it was dark. The overcast had disappeared. She stared out of the rounded windows at a pitch-black sky studded with millions of diamond stars and felt slightly like Lois Lane flying with Superman out into the wild blue yonder.

Except that Superman was really Everett in a miraculously restored suit and crisp white shirt. His tie had been replaced with a perfectly knotted black one, and gold cufflinks blinked from the smart French cuffs. How beautiful they looked together. She wasn't being conceited; they really did. She'd splurged her treasured supply of water on a shampoo she didn't really need. But it was nothing but the best for the one good dress she'd brought with her—a classic black, high-necked and long-sleeved, accented only with a single strand of pearls. Her earrings were tiny diamonds Mildred and the boys had given her for Christmas, and her coat was passable for evening wear. She looked good, smelled good, and felt good, despite the wretched beginning of the day. It was about to end magnificently.

The Barcelona Opera company, supported avidly by its patrons, was not an overly large group. But it had a regular season and performed quite credible works. It occurred to Jenny, as she strolled confidently through the theater on Everett's arm, that operagoers weren't so different throughout the world. They still dressed well, clustered in small groups to argue over music and personalities, and offered their criticism and compliments with the same libelous fervor.

The seats Everett had been so fortuitously gifted

with were, luckily, excellent ones. She and Everett graciously begged pardon as they squeezed past several people who were already seated. They took their places in the center section, some rows beyond the orchestra pit. The musicians were warming up with the usual cacophony, which Jenny loved to hear. Bows were being rosined, reeds soaked, and saliva blown out of brass horns. She observed them adjusting their pit lights upon their stands and checking through their music to make sure everything was in order.

She snuggled happily against Everett's arm after he helped her off with her coat. "You really surprise me, Everett. When did you become an opera buff?"

Everett glanced behind himself at a woman who had brought her jeweled binoculars with her. She gave the unnerving impression of penetrating into the back of his head and reading his thoughts.

He shifted to one hip in his seat. "To tell you the truth," he whispered over the floating fragments of music and talking, "I never did."

A full second passed before his words really soaked in. "You mean . . ." she hissed, "that—"

He held a quietening finger to his lips.

She lowered her voice. "You mean you brought me here tonight when it . . . it—"

"Bores me to death." His grin was sheepish. "Yep. But don't worry about it. I would've developed a rabid interest in firing squads if you'd said you wanted to see one."

She dropped her forehead to the heel of her hand. "I feel like an idiot."

"Well, you don't look like one." He placed an indiscreet hand on the swell of her thigh. His thumb sultrily caressed the length of muscle running up from her knee. "You don't feel like one, either."

"Don't add that to your crimes," she scolded playfully, and brushed his hand away. His sweetness came at the most inopportune times; she wished dizzily that he would kiss her.

Everett tucked his chastised hand across his waist inside his suitcoat. "You're safe," he said, and slumped lower on his spine. When she didn't reply, he added devilishly, "But don't get overconfident. It's early yet."

"This night may turn out to be more memorable than I thought." She smothered a smile, then put on an extremely artistic look. "Well, Everett, since we're here, high-handed pretenses and all, and there're a few minutes until the overture, it's time you became cultured. You *do* know who composed *Carmen*, don't you?"

A lovable ignorance spread over his face, only accentuating the handsomeness that she was growing all too aware of. "I haven't the foggiest," he said blissfully.

"Bizet."

"Oh."

"Do you know who Bizet was?"

"Nope."

"Well." Jenny sighed, and unceremoniously pushed his arm off her armrest and braced her elbow there. "My guess is that you would've liked him. He was known to have said, upon one occasion at least, that Mozart's music made him unwell, and certain things about Rossini's did the same. And that Haydn put him to sleep."

Everett laughed, interested not so much in what she was saying but that her leg was crossed conveniently near his hand. By cleverly manipulating the hem of her dress, he could smooth his palm along the swell of her calf. When he did, she jumped.

Jenny gave him a narrow-eyed scold, enjoying herself. "Learn a lesson from poor Carmen, Everett. Her lover was driven to tragic lengths because of his lust."

It was too late for Everett to think of an appropriate comeback. The lights were going down, and the orchestra was receiving the oboe's *A* to tune.

"Shh!" She leaned so near she could smell his after-shave. Her breath caught, and she became still for such stunning seconds that his eyes flicked to hers. "It . . . ah, it's time for the overture," she finished feebly.

Everett thought, when he leaned back for an unimpeded view of her breasts straining against the black georgette dress, that he would die from wanting this woman.

The applause at the end of Act One was deafening. Everett and Jenny clapped and cheered along with the rest. Carmen had been magnificent, even if she was a bit overweight and taller than poor, skinny Don José.

"Wasn't it wonderful?" Jenny nearly had to shout at him over the cheering.

His reply was drowned in the applause.

Jenny didn't hear what he said. She bent her head nearer and offered her ear. "What did you say?"

"I said, I love you."

The cheering ceased. The people disappeared from before and behind and from the sides. They weren't even in the theater any longer, but beneath a cool green willow in the springtime on an old street far outside Atlanta, Georgia.

"Did you hear what I said?" he asked her, eyes searching down at her, his wistful yearning drawing his brows together.

"Yes." Her lips hardly moved.

"Let's get out of here."

"Yes."

They walked for hours without noticing the cold, without thinking of work or what time it was. They passed through the cabaret-packed district south of the Ramblas and never heard the rowdiness of Gypsy joints or saw the prostitutes picking up their clients. They strolled hand-in-hand down the Ramblas, and there, on the boulevard of cafes and bars, they laughed at each other and remembered Dairy Queen sundaes and root beer floats and picnics with barbecued chicken.

"I'm starving," Everett said, hugging her.

"That's not a tiger you hear," she teased, hugging him back. "That's my stomach."

"What d'you want to eat?"

"Everything."

He bought paella with rice, beans, artichokes, peas, cauliflower, and a delicious sauce. After two glasses of Haute-Brion they were both sated and Jenny was deliciously light-headed.

They talked about everyone they knew. They cuddled on the cable car that swung out over the Mediterranean harbor to Montjuich. They held hands as they gazed down at Barcelona sparkling in her jeweled splendor at their feet. Everett took her in his arms.

Jenny made herself accessible to his most subtle moves, fitting into the crook of his arm and letting her breasts flatten against the hard magnificence of his chest. His hand fit naturally to the base of her spine. Her lips, when she offered them, were parted and anxious to convey a thousand things she could never find the words to say.

They drifted in tastes and textures and sighs that went nowhere and everywhere.

When Everett lifted his head at last, he didn't let

Jenny tumble into his eyes. He threaded his fingers deep in the mass of her curls at her nape and held her cheek pressed to his.

"Don't go," he muttered hoarsely as he held her head still.

She tried to stir. "Ev—"

"Don't go. Don't go back home, Jenny."

"But . . ."

"Stay here," his words rushed against her ear. "Just a few more weeks." She could feel his heart throbbing against her shoulder. She tried to turn in his arms, wanting to make him see, wanting to understand.

He kept her pinned, immobile, against him. He told her quickly what he'd been wanting to say all evening. "I know the reasons you're going to give me—the boys, your job. But I'll only be here for a couple more weeks, three at the most. Don't go, please."

It was what she'd wanted from him—that need, that magical pain that couldn't bear separation. But she wasn't as free to come and go as he was. Dragging her hand free, Jenny felt for the ledge of his jaw. The stubble was rough against her palm. People were wandering in and around them. She didn't care.

"I wish you'd ask me something easy."

"I'm not easy," he said. "I wish I was easy."

"I have to go home, Everett. I . . ."

He held her back from him then and lovingly searched her face. He shook his head. "How will I smile when you're gone, Jenny? How will I get up in the mornings? How will I do anything when you're not with me?"

Jenny's heart wouldn't listen to her head. It was breaking for him. Whoever said love was glory? It was a painful, painful process of never having enough, of fearing to lose.

"No one else could do this to me," she said against his shoulder, gazing out at the darkness.

"Do what, darling?"

"Tear me apart inside."

Something sparked inside him—the knowledge that loving was the exquisite agony of watching a person walk away with no assurances, of trusting that the time would come when you'd be together again. He knew he would have to let her go home.

Unable to swallow down the knot that was growing huge in his throat, he stepped back from her. His love was all over him.

Jenny knew a thrill that made her want to sing and weep at the same time.

"Well," he said, pretending a lightness neither of them felt, "you'll just have to give me the second best thing."

She cupped his jaw in her palm. "What could I ever give to you, my beautiful man?"

"Tell me out loud that you love me. I know you do, but tonight"—he looked away and blinked rapidly—"tonight I need to hear it."

Jenny caught the skirt of her dress as the wind ballooned it out. She drew her coat closer about her and averted her face so that he couldn't see the rawness that she feared showed in her eyes. Letting him see that would be fatal. No one should see that much.

"I never stopped, Everett." She looked at her shoes and let the words come slowly, one after another—the words that she had never had the courage to face before.

"For all those years, when I bore my sons and was a wife to Martin . . . I never stopped. There were times I thought I could learn to hate you for what you'd done. But that was only a game I played with myself because

I'd lost you. I . . . I never—" The tears welled. "It was so unfair to Martin, but I never lived through a day when I didn't love you."

When she looked back after a long pause, the lights from below caught Everett's face in their crossfire. A single glistening runnel of tears traced down each cheek and grew dim at the edges of his mouth. She knew he didn't care that she saw. He didn't speak to her for a while, long enough for them both to regret the years that could have been.

Then, out of the depths of a love that had been kept inside for many, many years, he said, "Will you come with me somewhere? I want to make love to you."

She never said the word *yes*. It was all in her eyes. He knew.

Not at any time did Jenny feel nervous about going with Everett to a strange hotel. Anyone with half an eye would have known they were lovers. But he didn't allude to the mechanical necessities of arrangements or inconveniences. He simply had her wait in the taxi, warm and secure, and when he returned he walked her easily to the elevator and smiled at her all the way up.

"Nervous?" he asked, grinning down at her as he unlocked the door. He pushed it open and stood waiting, dreading that she would change her mind at the last minute and say she couldn't do it.

She laughed a bit breathlessly as she stared at the darkened interior. "Yes. Are you?"

Everett led her inside and flipped a light switch as he shut the door. A warm glow settled over a beautifully appointed suite—inviting velours and brocades and dark, gleaming wood.

"Yes." He slipped her coat from off her shoulders. "But not for the reasons you think."

His need for her was so intense when he took her in

his arms, letting her coat fall about their feet, that Jenny thought he would begin undressing her. Without kissing her, though, he tucked his chin low and coaxed her to lift her eyes. His scent was blending with that of flowers somewhere, and it was a potent, drugging smell.

"Do you think me a lecher, Jenny?" he smiled down at her. "So starving for your flesh that I'd strip you naked the moment the lock slid into place?"

She flushed beautifully. "I thought you might have a tendency in that direction, yes."

"Then," he brushed his lips across hers, wispily, hauntingly, "think again, my darling. I've come courting."

Letting her go, he scooped up her coat and draped it over the back of a Windsor chair. She watched him unbutton his suit coat, then the top button of his shirt. He wrenched his tie askew. He strolled gracefully and unhurriedly to a stereo built into the wall and searched through the stations. Passing one that caught his ear, he moved the dial back. It was orchestrated music, not American, but easy and sensuously blue. He ambled about the room, pulling the drapes aside and glancing down. When he turned back unexpectedly, she was looking at the cut of his trousers, and her eyes fell to the contour of his crotch. He wanted her. Reflexively her eyes jerked away.

She knew by his smile that he'd seen, but it hardly mattered. He'd been mentally undressing her the last half hour.

"I can't remember the last time we danced," he said, and opened his arms in an invitation to come to him.

Jenny moved in his arms as if this were all a dream. And when his mouth slowly fastened to hers, parting her lips, which were already trembling with ready desire, she whimpered throatily. *Take me now,* her mind begged him. *I don't want to wait.*

But he forced the pace to one of infinite leisure. She stood nestled in his arms until a knock interrupted them.

"Your champagne, señor," the waiter said from a discreet distance.

Money exchanged hands and the small round table with its icy treasure was left just inside the door.

Jenny didn't want champagne. She wanted Everett, and it occurred to her now, observing his hands, that he didn't want champagne, either. But it was necessary—something to do to keep the evening from bursting out of control.

The bottle cork didn't go spinning off toward the ceiling like in the movies. Everett turned the glasses right-side up and poured the liquid in a soft, gurgling waterfall. Then, flicking off all but one lamplight as he approached, he placed the glass in her hand.

"What shall we drink to?" he asked lazily, and motioned her to the carpet before the stereo. "To Spain? To us? To days gone by?"

A knowing smile curved up the edges of Jenny's lips. She was aching all over. Her breasts were throbbing and tight with longing to be touched. The center of her pulsed, heavy and unbearable. He was playing her, she thought as he tossed some pillows to the floor—sharpening her, whetting her like some blade.

She laughed quietly. "I'm trying to think of something terribly clever, to make you laugh and think how lucky you are."

"And you think I don't know that?"

"Sometimes, I . . ." If he knew, couldn't he see that she only wanted to spend what was left of her life with him? She felt as if she were being pared, like an apple.

"Sometimes I think I think too much," she said hastily, and sipped her champagne.

She crossed her legs when she dropped to the floor and savored the beauty of him as he sipped and nestled his glass in his palm, the way he bowed his back against the wall to brace it, the length of his legs and the neatness of his ankles as they crossed. His suit coat hung open and its skirt crumpled heedlessly upon the carpet. How like him, she thought. Even with his virility, even with his passion that could blaze as violently as an inferno, even with his vulnerability that was as great as her own at times, he was oddly at ease with himself. He had told her he loved her. He had exposed that one primordial nerve of his being for the first time. And . . . it dawned on her now . . . he wasn't at ease; he was waiting. He needed for her to make an aggressive move.

Everett thought he knew the exact second when Jenny read his mind. He lay watching her beneath thickly fringed lashes. So much was happening inside him that he hardly had a handle on any of it. He'd been so furious when he'd learned how Ruth had hurt her, for a moment he thought he could have killed her. And then he remembered that he'd hurt Jenny too. Many years ago, much worse. Perhaps that's why he wanted Jenny to come to him now, of her own free will, to tell him by that very act that she'd forgiven him everything. He needed to be certain that she understood the point on the map where their courses would ultimately intersect. And where was that point? Was he thinking of marriage again? Had he come that far on this uncharted journey?

She rose and placed her glass on a table. Everett felt his pulses thicken as her arm reached behind her for the zipper to the filmy dress she wore. It whispered free and his groin tightened.

Keeping her head demurely bent, she undid the tiny buttons on the sides of her sleeves. The dress slipped off her shoulders as easily as the last of his champagne was drained from the glass.

It occurred to Everett that perhaps he was playing a fool's game when he saw the filmy black slip. He was already imagining the whiteness of her skin beneath her bra, the shadow beneath the sheer black stockings.

With a quick, graceful motion she shrugged off the slip. Then she lifted her eyes and he was stunned by the anguish in them.

"It should be easier, not harder, shouldn't it?" she choked around burgeoning tears.

He was holding her in an instant, cradling her to him as if she were fragile, spun silk.

"Ah, darling girl," he crooned, and rocked her back and forth. He smoothed her hair and whispered into it. "Ruth was right. I'm a bastard. I'm afraid I always have been."

"No, no," she protested against his chest. "You can't imagine the things I would like to do to you."

He laughed deep in his chest, a loving, totally sympathetic laugh.

Jenny wrapped her arms tightly about his chest, thankful for the anonymity of hiding her face as she talked. "I've lain awake at night and . . . done *everything* in my fantasies with you. But when I need the nerve, I . . ."

He nibbled the nape of her neck and sent showers of sparks cascading down her back. "One can stockpile an awful lot of inhibitions in eight years," he murmured, adoring the view of her hips in her pantyhose.

"Please," she said, pulling back her head, pressing herself against the straining masculine angles below his waist, "I've come for you. Take me."

Everett found he could not finish the drama he'd

chosen to play. And he feared, once he began to rid himself of his clothes, that he couldn't last long enough to get that done. With the most acute pleasure he thought he'd ever known, he saw she was as frenzied as he was. She fought the buckle of his belt and hurled it from him with a word he'd never heard her say before. He laughed. And when he'd kicked his trousers, heaven knew where, she knelt over him, naked and bewitching, restraining him the way the moon bargains with the sun during those misty moments before dawn.

His pressure mounted, wonderful and intense. He told her with his breaths, ragged and distorted, that he couldn't bear for long what she was doing to him. She seemed to know when the tension was ready to break, for she turned on her back and opened her arms.

"Do you really love me?" she said, eyes glistening with her own love.

He couldn't look at her. He couldn't focus his eyes. He pressed his mouth against the curls at her temple. His tongue touched her ear.

"Yes," he groaned out the word. "My love comes from me to you. Hold me very tight, sweet love." He knew, in those rending, splintering moments, that he didn't want to face the rest of his life without her.

Taking the final steps to the truth took Jenny another day and a half. At four o'clock in the morning, on the day she was scheduled to leave Spain, she tossed on her single bed in the motor home. She got up and turned on the light. She knew the curse she was under. She'd known it from the moment that Everett had stood on that hill in Montjuich with tears in his eyes. She had to tell him the whole truth of what he was, of what Ruth had done to him.

When daylight came she would leave here. She couldn't go with a lie between them.

Repairing herself as well as she could, putting on a fresh sweater with her slacks, she brushed her hair. She applied fresh lipstick and a bit of blusher. She hadn't slept at all, and her eyes felt full of sand. She fetched her coat from where it lay across her bags, which were already packed. Finding a flashlight, she tediously picked her way across the boardwalk and made for the office building a good city block away.

Because of the telephone situation Everett had bunked in one of the offices from their arrival. She had no idea which one. She'd never had a reason to come here before. Most of the office lights were dark, and the outside floodlights threw spooky shadows across the front. Two rooms were alight.

She nodded to the security guard at the outside door and showed her ID. "I need to use the telephone," she fibbed in horrendous Spanish.

He pulled his collar a bit higher on his neck. "Keep to the left, señora."

She leaned against the door. At least the building was well heated over here, she thought, and turned left at the first hallway.

Stopping at the first lighted office she came to, she knocked on the door.

"Come in," someone barked in English.

She poked the upper half of her body inside, keeping what she hoped was an innocent look upon her face.

An older man sat at a desk, studying an atlas. He looked up with sandy, questioning brows. "May I help you?"

"Mr. Black's office?"

He gave her an odd look, then smiled. "Down to the end of the hall. Take a right."

What was he thinking?

"Thank you," she said quickly.

"You're welcome. Close the door when you go out."

Rude! Beginning to question her judgment in coming, Jenny plodded down the hall and turned right. Six doors lined the wall, but only one had a light on behind a panel of textured glass. It had to be Everett's. Now that she'd found him, dear God, how could she tell him what she had to say?

She tried the knob, halfway expecting it to be locked. "Everett?" she whispered.

From behind another door she heard faint strains of . . . what, Mozart? Was he listening to the radio? It took as much courage as she could summon to tap her knuckles upon the wooden door frame. She waited.

Nothing.

Then she opened it a crack. "Everett?"

Perhaps it was the rustle of someone moving that prompted Jenny to enter. It was unlike her, walking in without being invited.

She moved through an outer office complete with carpet and a small jungle of potted plants. There was the smell unique to a closed place of business—paper, duplicating fluid, glue. Through an open doorway, the one through which the Mozart drifted, a light burned brightly.

By moving only a few feet she could see Everett with his socked feet propped on a hassock. Several open ledgers were spread on a table before him. His chest was bare, and he wore tattered jeans zipped to the waist but unsnapped. The curls upon his chest created a dark shadow that tapered to nothing and disappeared below the waist of his trousers. A tray of half-eaten food cluttered the carpet at his feet. He was deep in thought, the tip of his tongue caught between his teeth, unaware of her presence.

Oh, Everett, if she could capture this moment and place it with all her other memories: Everett in cutoff jeans, mowing the lawn; Everett tipping back his head and killing off a soft drink; Everett walking across a street, a sweater looped about his neck by its arms, his eyes crinkling, his teeth flashing in a laugh; Everett saying he loved her on a hillside in Montjuich.

He stopped in his study for a moment, remaining perfectly still and looking at nothing. Lifting his head abruptly, he saw her.

"Jenny," he breathed and came to his feet.

Enormously timid now that she was here, Jenny pressed her fingers to her lips. She stayed where she was; her feet seemed strangely wooden.

"I hope you don't mind."

"Mind?" His eyes welcomed her with their blue warmth. "Of course I don't mind."

She let him close his hands about her wrists. It was there again—the painful, aching longing to be close to him, to be the most important thing in his world. She knew he was feeling it as much as she.

"I couldn't sleep, Everett. I wanted to talk to you before I go."

"I'm so glad you came," he said against her forehead as he folded her gently into his arms.

As his lips came down hard upon hers, all her reluctance disappeared. The truth would be all right now. Whatever happened, she would help him through it. She let Everett play out the kiss, which evolved into dozens of tiny rough kisses all over her face. She laughed softly and held him tightly about his neck. He nuzzled the back of her neck, and as she stood on tiptoe, her chin buried in his shoulder, a shadow moved somewhere to her right.

Jenny sensed the presence of someone else rather than really saw it. Her mind cleared perfectly, and she was aware of herself thinking, *Someone is in the room. He isn't alone.*

But to turn, to detach herself from his arms and to see Ruth wrapped in a sheet that was tucked tightly above her breasts, her face free of makeup and her lips smiling with private triumph, knocked the breath from Jenny's body. It wasn't real. She was dreaming. Ruth wasn't here with her long blond hair streaming about her shoulders, her bare feet gleaming mockingly from beneath the sheet. It wasn't real! It wasn't fair!

She felt her jaw go loose with horror.

"Darling," Ruth drawled lazily, "you didn't tell me Jennifer was coming over."

Everett made a sound deep in his throat.

In her daze Jenny wondered if he would actually have the audacity to try and lie his way out of it. Panic thrummed in her ears, deafening her. She doubted she could have heard anything he said. Then a dangerous, black hatred wrapped its arms about her like a shroud. The room, the building—all of it seemed covered with the thick, viscous mud outside.

All the Black women are doomed to heartache. Heartache? What was heartache compared to living death?

Then Jenny quit thinking at all. She didn't run out of the building. She walked. With precise steps she passed the rude man's door, out past the security guard, and across the lawn to her boardwalk. She saw everything happening with remarkable clarity: the helicopter that would take her to Barcelona, the money that Everett would send her in an envelope so that they wouldn't have to torture themselves by meeting face to face.

She knew she would never see him again. And now, feeling the cold in a live, cruel way, she knew she couldn't think about it. She was going home. She would be Scarlett O'Hara. She would think about it tomorrow. She had the rest of her life to think.

Chapter Nine

"I'm too old to trade valentines at school, Mother."
Stephen made a gruesome face. He leaned over Jenny's
shoulder and presented her with a mimeographed note
from his teacher. "That's kid stuff."

Dinner at the Howard house was finished and cleared
away. It was the unhurried lull between the six o'clock
news and homework and baths. The boys, sprawled on
the carpet amid a clutter of books and model planes,
had been arguing over whose shower had to be first.
Mildred, tired, was dozing in her recliner. Jenny was in
one of her increasingly compulsive flurries since returning from Spain. She had spread out her "bring home"
work on the dining room table—a great portfolio and a
half-dozen cylinder cases. Tonight, she promised herself, would be different; she wouldn't go to bed until
she was too tired to even think. Tonight she wouldn't
cry.

Stephen smoothed his note upon a large sheet of

Jenny's Mylar paper. "See? A party with cookies. All the girls'll make goo-goo eyes and everything. Yucckh!"

"You don't like goo-goo eyes, Stephen?" laughed Jenny.

"He'll outgrow it, Mom." Jeffrey's sibling guarantee came from behind an algebra book he was reading on his own. His handsome face popped into view above the book.

"Listen, Darth Vader . . ." Stephen began.

Jeffrey, throwing his voice into a girlish falsetto, giggled. He fluttered his eyelashes like an amorous cartoon character. "Oh, Stevie, I love you."

Jenny was accustomed to the banter of her children, but tonight she wished for a little peace and quiet. Her brows drew into a scowl.

Stephen said, "Shut up, Jeff, before I knock your block down the street." He thought a moment, then chuckled at his own joke. "Block down the street," he explained. "Get it? *Block* down the *street.*"

"Stephen," groaned his mother.

"I'll tell Tammy, I'll tell Tammy," Jeffrey chanted. "Ask him what he was doing with Tammy behind the bus stop, Mother."

"Shut up, Jeff."

"Kissing Tammy Weinmuller." Jeffrey placed a hand over his heart and pretended to swoon. "Oh, Stevie baby, will you give me a valentine? Please, please? A big one, with crinkly red things on it?"

Making a sound like a fire engine winding up its siren, Stephen barreled into the living room and sent the first thing he found sailing at his brother's head. It was a throw pillow. Which, in turn, sent Jeffrey's algebra book flying through the air at Stephen. Jeffrey was weary of the confines of winter; he was ready for a royal tussle. Grabbing his brother, they went rolling across the floor in an inelegant display of arms and legs. Stephen wound up crumpled upon his grandmother's feet.

Mildred's head came up. "Boys, boys! Stop that scuffling this instant!"

Jenny, appearing in the doorway from the dining room, stood with a fist braced on her hip. She was wearing jeans and a gray zippered sweat shirt. She looked more like their sister than their mother. Yet, as she stood in perfect maternal authority, her presence overpowered the boys' short-lived attack of cabin fever.

Mildred sighed fondly as her grandsons came to attention. "What do you do with wild horses?"

"You keep 'em in a barn," Jenny replied, trying not to smile.

She bent for the throw pillow and replaced it on the sofa. Pointing at the book, she gestured for Jeffrey to pick it up. "We're outgrowing this house, boys. Now, please, keep it down. Broken windows and damaged Sheetrock are things I don't need right now."

"You said we were outgrowing the house last year," Mildred reminded, "when you and Ray were looking at house plans."

The mention of Ray raised a number of questions for Mildred, all of them disheartening. Since returning from Spain, Jenny had broken things off with the banker. The only reason she gave for it was that she "just had to." She'd been working overtime with a frenzy. Late at night she'd seen the light leaking beneath Jenny's door and had tapped.

"It's late, daughter," she would remind softly. She hoped Jenny would call her in to confide what was worrying her, but she never did.

"Sleep well, dear," she would call disappointedly, and go on to bed.

Then Mildred would lie awake, wondering what disturbing thing had happened to her daughter in Spain. Jenny's comments had been so sketchy and ambiguous. She'd sworn the trip was not only profitable for Chase Interiors but for her. But in the same breath a grim bleakness would drift across her face. She would seem remote, oblivious to everything. A person had to call her name several times just to get her attention. She'd lost weight and often refused to eat anything at all. Only one thing would devastate Jenny like that: Everett Black. Mildred could wring his treacherous neck.

"I'm thinking of talking to a few realtors again," Jenny was saying, as if it had just occurred to her. "What d'you think, guys? Wouldn't it be nice to find a place and work on it during the summer?"

"I like it here," Stephen threw in.

Jeffrey glared at him. "You'd like it anywhere, dopey. It'd be fine, Mom. It'd give us something to do beside watch *I Love Lucy* all summer. I thought you couldn't get a loan."

Jenny absently ran the top of her zipper up and down. Jeffrey attacked problems too much like an adult. "I wasn't talking about the kinds of plans we made about the house on Ferris—the shop and everything. Something on a smaller scale. Maybe a run-down old farm in the country. You boys could clean up the outside and I could handle the inside. A few cans of paint and a yard or two of gingham can do a world of good. What d'you think, Mother?"

Mildred was working on a different wavelength. "I was by the old house a few days ago," she mused, her hands folded in her lap. "After the For Sale sign went down, I thought we'd see things happening to it. But no one's moved in, and no one's torn it down."

Plucking tiredly at a curl, Jenny said, "Maybe whoever bought it has had second thoughts."

Mildred shrugged. "I really should forget the old place. But, you know, having lived there for so many years, raising you there, I can't help but kind of keep an eye on it."

"Maybe they'd like to sell it back," Jeffrey suggested from behind his book.

"Then they'd have another sign up, jerk," said Stephen with friendly rudeness.

Jenny pointed her finger at her smiling younger son. "Don't call names. And they wouldn't necessarily have a sign up." She drew her mouth into a pucker and met her mother's watchful eyes. "Maybe I'll call First Mark and see if they know anything about it. Just on the outside chance—"

"Don't."

"What's the harm?"

"You'll just get your hopes up all over again. It's just not worth it, dear. I didn't mean to start something. I'm sorry."

"When's Everett coming back?" Jeffrey asked like a shot blasting out of the dark. "I've been practicing Pac-Man. Mom, couldn't we get a video game to put on the TV?"

There had been times when Jenny's children had caught her off guard, but never like this, never with this heart-stopping accuracy. For a full five seconds she stood without moving, her features so frozen they looked as if they'd crack. Why had he asked about Everett?

Mildred took one look at Jenny and had her worst fears of Everett confirmed. Quickly, a bit panic-struck, she pushed out of her chair and began straightening the room.

"The man is an adult, Jeffrey," Mildred said sternly. "You should call him Mr. Black."

Jeffrey didn't understand his blunder. "But he told me to call him Everett."

"My, my," Mildred pretended to fuss over the room. "If I weren't here to pick up after you children, you'd have to shovel your way into this room. Stephen, this sweater has been here for two days."

The older woman gathered up several items, yawned, and said she was too tired to stay up any longer. All three of them watched her leave, stoop-shouldered and weary.

Jeffrey, his beauty marred by his anxiety, looked at his mother. "What'd I do? All I said was—"

Returning to her work at the dining room table, Jenny twisted at a pencil, gouging her nails into the soft wood. "Nothing, Jeffrey. Don't worry about it."

The boy roamed aimlessly about the dining room for a moment. He picked up a drawing, looked at it, and laid it down. "You're not going to marry Ray, are you?"

The pencil snapped with an alarming pop. Jeffrey's eyes darted to hers, and Jenny shook her head. She dropped the broken pieces on the table. "Would that be so bad, darling? Couldn't you learn to live with it if I did?"

Jeffrey glanced toward Stephen, who was sprawled on his stomach before the television. His mouth hardened in stubbornness. "It's none of my business, you mean."

Feeling kicked in the stomach, Jenny slumped a little. "Don't be so much like me. Of course it's your business. The man would be your father. You have rights to your opinion, just like anyone else."

The impetuousness in Jeffrey caused his forehead to crinkle. He straightened the stack of drawings, then thumped the top ones, sending them skittering across the table. "Then why don't you marry someone like Everett, Mom? He's cool. Ray doesn't care nothin' about Stevie and me."

Jenny felt, when she saw tears sparkling heatedly in Jeffrey's eyes, that her heart would break. Skirting the table, she stepped near her beautiful ten-year-old. He was trying bravely not to cry. Crying had been beneath his dignity of late.

"Come," she said, opening her arms.

He shook his head. "I'm too old for that stuff."

She smiled. "No one's too old for this stuff." She closed her arms about him and felt the warmth of satisfaction when he clung to her a little desperately. He needed a father. In his heart of hearts he was crying out for a pillar of strength, for help to cope with weaknesses he didn't even recognize yet.

"Oh, Jeffrey," she whispered into the silky crown of his head, "sometimes I forget you're not all grown up."

"Yes I am."

She held him tightly. "Then you have to trust me. I won't do anything that would make you unhappy."

"Promise?" he snuffled.

"I promise."

Jeffrey returned her hug. He sighed against her collarbone. "But it would be nice to have a daddy who could make three hundred thousand at Pac-Man, Mom."

Oh, God, the unwitting cruelties of children!

"I know," she choked so softly, the implications were lost on Jeffrey. She gave his shoulder a squeeze and watched him saunter back to the living room. He would break her heart, she thought. Every time he would break her heart.

The boys settled down to their reading and homework and Jenny stood over the table, staring blindly at nothing. Her life was slipping through her fingers. Perhaps she could get a grip on things now that her pregnancy scare was over. Or at least she was ninety-nine percent certain it was over. Things hadn't been quite normal during her last cycle, but that was to be expected, wasn't it? Her emotional state had been near the breaking point when she'd come home and was two weeks late.

With that behind her now, she could bend her energies to falling out of love with Everett. Work was the answer—hard work and lots of it. She would devote herself to it and to her children. Then she wouldn't keep remembering the words Everett had said and the things he had done. Why couldn't Ray have been like Everett? Why couldn't she have felt anything when Ray had kissed her? Should she try one more time? Now that it was over with Everett? She just couldn't.

She gazed at the boys stretched blissfully on the carpet. Jeffrey's jeans were at his ankles again, and Stephen's tennis shoes were coming apart at the soles. She had plenty of places to spend her money without thinking about houses and new neighborhoods again too. But perhaps she needed that along with the work. What would be the harm in just driving down Ferris Street in the next week or so? She had to have something to hope for besides a life without Everett. Looking was still free. And that was all she would do—take one look from the car.

She lowered herself into the chair and picked up her design. She didn't even see it. Instead she saw Ruth Black's laughing green eyes. Dear God, she had to get over this thing!

The first day of March proved to be pleasant weatherwise. The month would probably come in like a lamb and blow out like a lion, Jenny thought. People were exulting in being able to walk down the street wearing light sweaters and jackets. Jenny had fished through her closet for a pleated skirt and a spring blouse and had topped it with a powder-blue sweater.

When she parked the car on Ferris Street, having taken two weeks to get up her courage, she took a deep breath of premature spring air. She smoothed her skirt as she leaned against the door of her Volkswagen and peered up at the old house.

"You promised to look from the car," she muttered out loud. But she paid no attention to herself and promptly walked up the sidewalk, past the willow tree, to the rambling old house.

Something about the place *was* odd, as Mildred had said. The acreage had been neatly cleaned and the shrubbery trimmed back. Even the edges of the sidewalk had been clipped. Forsythia tried its level best to pop into bloom. Here and there brave sprigs of green grass poked out of the ground. On the side of the porch leaned the For Sale signs that First Mark had never picked up. A look of tidiness permeated the grounds, an expectancy, yet no sign of life existed anywhere: no car tracks, no items moved into the house, no electricity turned on—nothing.

It was unfair, Jenny thought with a strange rush of possessiveness. Her first impulse must be right. The buyer was planning to clean it up a bit and put it back on the market in the hopes of making a spring profit, shifting it from family to family like an unwanted foster child.

Still absorbed, she walked into the office of Chase Interiors and nodded an absent hello to Pamela. Her superior was already buried in a stack of drawings. Her cup of coffee sent up its cheery curl of steam beside the telephone, the receiver of which was pinched between shoulder and ear.

Before Jenny took off her jacket, she found Esther Simmons's number in the directory and dialed.

"First Mark Realty," came a bored, nasal voice. "This is Diane. May I help you?"

"Esther Simmons, please."

Jenny traced the outline of Everett's name as she waited. When it dawned on her what she was doing, she scratched a series of lines through it. Then, as if that didn't exorcise the ghost of him thoroughly enough, she ripped off the page and crumpled it viciously. She hurled it at her wastebasket, missed, and dropped into her chair, depressed.

"Esther Simmons. What may I do for you?"

"Ah, yes, Ms. Simmons. I have a question about the old three-story house on Ferris Street. First Mark had it listed this past January."

"I remember the place."

"I was driving by today. I noticed the signs were down but not picked up. Can you tell me anything about it?"

There was a slight pause and the sound of ruffling papers. Esther coughed and begged pardon for taking so long. "What did you say your name was, Miss . . ."

Jenny smiled as she recalled Esther's mistake about her being Mrs. Black. Everett had kissed her that day. Her smile faded instantly.

"Mrs. Howard," she said crisply. "You probably don't remember me."

"I'm sorry, I meet so many. Well, I see according to my records, Mrs. Howard, that the property really was sold. I don't have any indication that we're going to relist it. I've just neglected to pick up the signs. Does that answer your question?"

No, it did not. "Could you tell me the purchaser? Perhaps I might approach them myself. I really did have hopes of buying that property, and since no one's moved in . . ."

The older woman chuckled. "For a property with as many problems as it had, it generated considerable interest. Let me see now. . . . Yes, the name on the contract is Black. A Mr. Everett Black."

Jenny felt the floor open beneath her feet. She was falling through it to some dark tomb. She had to remember—quickly, hatefully, unfairly—the reasons why she was better off without Everett. He was trouble. He was lies. She didn't need him. She hated him!

She saw Pamela looking at her with puzzled eyes. She was covering her receiver. "Jenny?"

She couldn't think yet. Everett had bought her house? Why?

"Jenny!"

Jenny jumped. Pamela and Esther Simmons spoke at the same time. She held out an imploring hand to Pamela.

"Oh, yes, Ms. Simmons. Forgive me. I was woolgathering. Do you happen to have a phone number where Mr. Black can be located? Something out of town, perhaps?" That was a dumb thing to say.

Esther made a sound of hunting through her file.

"Nooo," she drew out the word, "there's nothing out of town, but I do show a local number. I suppose it's all right to let you have it. I might say in passing, Mrs. Howard, if you plan to try and purchase the house, I can probably help you by handling the transaction through the business. That is, if Mr. Black wishes to sell."

Jenny mumbled some unintelligible remark about making sure she passed that information along to Mr.

Black. "I'm ready for the number now," she prompted. Her hand was shaking so badly, she broke her pencil lead and scrambled to find another.

"Actually it's a hotel. The Bentley. Downtown."

The Bentley! What in heaven's name would Everett be doing at the Bentley? In Atlanta?

"Thank you," she said from far, far away.

The silence in the office was lengthy and unreal. In some insane attempt to reclaim a sense of the present, Jenny walked to the coffee maker. She picked up a cup, stood looking at it for a moment, then put it down. Turning away, she remembered what she'd come for. She poured out a cup.

"You've had a distressing conversation," Pamela said.

Jenny dipped her spoon into the sugar and watched it slide off the edge of her spoon. She never took sugar.

"Do you want to tell me your bad news, then I'll tell you my good?" suggested the other woman. "It's about you."

Tasting the coffee, Jenny sighed and poured it out. "It had better be a commission to redecorate the White House."

Pamela laughed. "Not quite, but almost."

"Really?" She heard herself speaking normally. This was actually happening. She was carrying on as if she weren't breaking to pieces inside. "It's my reputation," she joked. "It tends to infiltrate this town. Like measles. Or fallout."

Rising, pouring another cup of coffee and placing it on the corner of Jenny's desk, Pamela rested one hip upon the corner. "Keep burying yourself deeper and deeper in your stubborn pride, Jenny. Don't tell me about it. I'm giving you the raise anyway."

The coffee scalded Jenny's mouth, and she sucked in her breath.

"You said the magic word," she choked, fanning herself. "What's happened?"

It wasn't often that Pamela bubbled. Though enormously competent, her personality was generally like the clothes she wore: conservative and dark-hued. But this time she tilted back her small head and laughed at the ceiling. She stretched her hands high.

"You are so good for me, Jenny! First that nice commission from the Spain job. Now someone . . ." She walked back to her desk and consulted a pad. "A firm by the name of Wells and Associates has offered us a fantastic job. Contingent upon your doing the work." She gave a ladylike salute. "My hat's off. Anything else I can get off."

"Well, I've always admired those shoes you're wearing."

Pamela laughed.

Good, thought Jenny. If she could just get out the next words. "If I asked you for an hour off," she tried flippancy, "would you take back the raise?"

Pamela pushed her sleeves back and began pulling books from a drawer of her desk. "Take anything you want, sweetie, but you have to drive by the place and make some kind of verbal contract before these angels change their minds. It's on Bellevue Street. Down at the west end."

"Bellevue? Where the old orphanage used to be?"

"Yep. They're going to revamp the entire thing and build a new building beside it as well. There must be thirty-five rooms in that old orphanage."

Jenny made a dreary calculation. Driving to the Bentley Hotel would have to wait until afternoon. Which was just as well; she wasn't ready to face Everett yet.

Nodding, rising to put some items in her attaché case, she bumped a vase on her desk. A pool of water spread mutinously over one end of her desk. It was a godsend—a tiny emergency to put things into perspective.

"Oh, dear!"

Snatching papers out of the way, she hurriedly began blotting up the water with a handful of Kleenex. Pamela was running for paper towels. The two women sopped up the mess, and when the last wet tissue and towel had been thrown in the wastebasket, Pamela stood quietly for a moment.

"Jenny, what's happened?"

Jenny kept her head down. "Would you believe me if I said I'm just a little tired?"

"No."

"It's partly true. I haven't been sleeping too well lately."

Not being a demonstrative woman, Pamela had difficulty touching Jenny. She placed her hand on the slender wrist. "Jenny, don't try to fool a veteran like me. I know man trouble when I see it. What's the matter? Ray giving you a hard time?"

"Oh, no." Jenny realized that Pamela didn't even know about Everett. "It's not Ray at all. There's . . ."

"Someone, though?"

Jenny nodded. "It's so involved."

"Men love to be involved."

"That's not true. Actually it's simple. I said I wanted marriage."

"And he wants an affair."

"Not exactly. Well, yes. Why shouldn't I want marriage, I want to know? What's wrong with that? I need to get married, Pamela. Everything would be so much easier. Jeffrey needs jeans and Stephen's out of his sneakers again. Oh, hell, that's not the reason. Why am I saying all that stuff?"

"It doesn't matter." Pamela released Jenny's wrist

and waved a finger back and forth before her face.
"Nothing is easier if you're married. Take it from me,
all problems can be solved, but if you're married, there
are two problems for every one."

"Yes, but your outlook is warped."

Pamela giggled. "I choose to say it's enlightened."

"And you're no one to give advice." Pamela was a
disaster with men. She had two divorces to her credit.
She approached marriage like she did her wardrobe—
conservative and dark-hued.

"I'm the perfect one to give advice." Pamela lavished
her counsel. "Have an affair with the man. Get it out of
your system. Or live with him and try it on for size. But
please, don't add fuel to the fire. *Don't get married,*
Jenny."

Jenny started packing her attaché case with the
items she would need for contracts, indicating that she
couldn't talk about it any longer.

"Maybe with my raise I'll be able to buy the house I
want," she said lightly. "I'll acquire the marks of an
unsatisfied woman. I'll involve myself with things."

Pamela smiled. "Before you make yourself a mental
case, drive out to Bellevue and talk to the people. Then
you can get your little dirty work done on your time off.
If you meet me at the Lunchbox at two o'clock, we can
eat late. Okay?"

"You're certainly in a celebrating mood."

"Celebrating, ha!" Pamela called as Jenny marched
out the door, case swinging. "We'll have a glass of wine
and I'll tell you about my second husband."

Bellevue was an old rambling street off the highway
running toward Atlanta. At one time the orphanage
had been set out in the boondocks. But with the expansion of Atlanta and the tendency of the smaller towns to
grow into it, this particular area was slowly filling with
industrial sites. Each of the new buildings had modern,

terraced grounds complete with trees and sprinkler systems and long, winding asphalt drives and parking areas. Still relatively uncluttered, it was one of the South's drawing cards for fresh northern capital.

Jenny hadn't driven out this way in a long time. Amazing how things could change, she thought. But then, sometimes it didn't take long for things to change: a day, a heartbeat.

On the radio Dionne Warwick was singing "Feelin' Old Feelin's Again." She snapped it off. She couldn't do that to herself. Not now.

Only five cars sat in the parking lot, plus a couple of vans bearing contractor's logos. But on the acreage beyond her, set in the distant trees, gleamed a massive cement slab. A dozen men browsed over its freshly poured surface.

Jenny made a quick inspection of herself in the rearview mirror. She fluffed at her hair, took up her case, and locked the car. Finding the office wouldn't be hard, she guessed. One good yell would hustle up someone.

It didn't take a yell. A woman with an English teacher's spine and marvelous cheekbones sat at a desk that, she hoped, would be one of the first things to go when the building was gutted. She could never have a back like that, thought Jenny, or those cheekbones. Perhaps if she had, Ruth wouldn't have hurt her so badly.

The front room was unfurnished, stark, as if waiting to be addressed. Even the window mourned their nakedness. She gave the woman her name and told her she was expected.

"I see," the woman replied in a surprisingly unteacherish voice. "Could you find your own way, honey, do you think? It's the third door on your left."

Jenny knocked on the third door on the left. When

no one answered she pushed it open. She called out. She'd learned her lesson about walking into rooms without making very, very sure they were unoccupied.

A bit uncourteous of the clients, really, not to be waiting for her. Oh, well, she could use a few minutes of absolute quiet. That would give her time to decide what to do about the house on Ferris. And "the Mr. Black" who had bought it.

She browsed from window to window. The room itself had been divested of all furniture except a functional desk and two plain chairs. She shouldn't, she told herself, pursue the matter of the house on Ferris Street any further. Obviously Everett had changed his mind about putting the research complex there. But the thoughts of letting it go so easily galled her. Was she kidding herself? Didn't she just want to see him again? Was she foolishly hoping that she would discover that it had all been some colossal mistake, that she hadn't seen what she'd seen?

How could she be doing this to herself again? she thought in disbelief. *Look at the lovely hardwood of this floor, Jennifer Howard. Look at the ten-foot ceilings and forget Everett Black.*

She threw her attaché case upon the desk and flipped the clasps open. The clatter echoed through the empty room.

Behind her the door whispered gently. A foot creaked on the threshhold.

Pasting on a breezy smile for the new client, Jenny swung around.

"This time you won't go until I say what I have to say," he said.

Chapter Ten

*I*n the instant of seeing Everett standing there, the door clicking shut behind him, Jenny reacted without thinking. "Everett," she breathed, and stepped toward him, wondering, thrilled, seeing nothing but his arms about her at last, his lips covering hers, his whispers healing the torn places in her soul.

And he, though marked with a vague uncertainty about her reaction, responded the same way. His need to take that step actually propelled him forward. Then reality blinded them: a bell in the dead of night, a flash in a pitch-black room.

Both of them stopped, smiles vanishing miserably, and let the doubts bind them until responses were impossible.

Everett leaned back against the door. He slumped with a discouraged sigh and braced the sole of one shoe against the baseboard. Letting his weight settle back upon his spine, his chest rose and fell, as if he had run a very long way and had no intentions of going one step farther.

"I thought I'd play the fool one more time." He looked about the room as if this moment were the culmination of a series of well-synchronized plans to destroy him.

"Three times are due a man," he added with a wry smile. "Like a cat's nine lives or something."

Jenny flailed unsuccessfully behind herself for a chair. Her confusion had no beginning and no end. What was going on here?

"Oh, no." She got the words out at last and pressed her fingers over her lips to keep them from quivering.

Without the customary suit and tie, Everett hardly looked like himself. His buff, pleated trousers brushed across the tops of sneakers that showed wear on the tops of the toes. His shirt was some blue thing in terry, V-necked and sensual, with a few sprigs of dark curls peeping from the ribbing. A wool sport jacket with tan patches on the sleeves swung open to reveal his lack of a belt through the loops. The effect was smartly unstudied, something men paid thousands of dollars to achieve. But he looked as if he hadn't slept or eaten a decent meal in days.

"I had a speech memorized," he said plaintively. "It's taken me this long to get it all together. After seeing the look on your face, I don't know whether to say it to you or myself."

"What . . . what are you doing here?" She dragged herself up until she stood straight.

"Ahh," he shook his head and looked at the floor, "that's a hard question. Heart above the head stuff? Business? Both or neither?" He threaded his fingers through his hair and clapped the back of his neck. His head came up. "Hell, how should I know? I've just bought the place. You look terrible, Jenny."

She didn't know whether to laugh or cry. "What did you expect?"

"A hello, maybe."

The despair of the past weeks threaded through her reply until it was more a breath than an answer. "I didn't think we'd ever say hello again."

His profile was elegant against the stark emptiness of the room. The silence spun out for a time. At length he said, "After you walked out that night, I wasn't sure I wanted to."

He blamed her, didn't he? Even now he blamed her. With his male justification he was turning it all around to make it her fault!

Tears collecting in her throat, she whirled to the desk and closed the top of her attaché case with a hurt, desperate slam.

The inflection of his voice didn't allow her to even snap it shut. "I would've thought you'd have a speech of your own all prepared," he challenged her. "What d'you say? I'll let you have the first shot, Jenny. Here's my chest. The old Black finesse is once again in working order. See?"

With both hands he pulled open his jacket and bared his sweater to whatever wounds she could inflict, verbal or otherwise.

She knew he was hurting, but so was she. She twisted the clasps of her case shut with shaking fingers. She grabbed up her purse, dropped it, and retrieved it. Tears stung her eyes badly now, and she kept her head down as she dragged her purse upon her shoulder and headed for the door, her case bumping against her legs.

"Shut up, Everett," she choked. "Just . . . shut up."

Everett came away from the wall as she swung around. Jenny heard his car keys jingle in his pocket and his sneakers swish mutely upon the hardwood floor.

"No, no, Jenny." He stepped between her and the door. He began forcibly prying the case from her hand, and when he had wrested it free, he tossed it to the floor without looking at it. It made a raucous clatter, skimming and scraping across the surface of the hardwood.

The violence didn't seem to faze him. He grasped her arms and lifted her up by the shoulders. His grip was agonizing and hopeless. Jenny's head arched far back, her eyes closed, and her throat stretched whitely in the shaft of sunshine pouring into the room.

"You're not closing me out again," he promised grittily, bending over her, shaking her. "Not without listening to my side of it. Look at me, Jenny!"

She was a limp doll beneath his bruising hands. "I don't have to look at you. I can hear you."

"Dammit, open your eyes! I want to know, once and for all, what happened to us."

Jenny could feel his breath. It was ragged and sweet. How could she tell him what had happened to them? She didn't truly know, herself. She dragged her eyes open with great effort.

"I'm not ready for this," she said with a dull, pleading honesty no one could have feigned. "I haven't had time to get ready for this, Everett."

Her wretchedness was so genuine that Everett stood for some seconds without moving or speaking, not even breathing. He gradually relaxed his hold of her. Slowly then, as if he were being held at gunpoint, he gently let her go and opened his hands wide, emptily, outward.

"Oh, you do have a way about you, Jenny Stephenson," he said with a rueful shake of his head. "I'll give you that."

"Howard," came the hoarse reply. "Jenny Howard."

"Jenny Howard, then. One and the same—sweetheart of Everett Black, widow of Martin Howard, mother of Jeffrey and Stephen Howard, lover of Everett Black . . ."

Jenny's life flashed back in sudden, fiery resilience, meeting his flint on flint, the spark falling upon dry, explosive tinder. She jerked around, sending the pleats of her skirt fluttering about her knees. Her shoulder struck his as she darted past him. And her heels, as she skimmed across the hardwood to the discarded attaché case, clicked a harsh denunciation of him and his truth.

Everett beat her there. He stepped between her and the case and shoved up his sleeves, jacket and all, as if he were preparing to do some ghastly destructive work if she tried to pick it up.

Jenny retreated, openmouthed and shivering.

His words grated. "Did I say something to finally touch you, Jenny Howard? Hmm? Did I chip through the brick wall you've built around yourself? Well, you were my lover, darling. You took and you gave. Oh, God, how you gave. And that gives me certain rights—"

She wanted to batter him with her fists, to beat him into silence. "It gives you nothing, Everett Black! No rights, no nothing!"

"Damned if it doesn't. I have the right to explain what you think you saw that night."

Jenny couldn't take this. It was ripping the heart right out of her. Like a frantic child she covered both ears and turned her head from side to side. Her shoulder bag slid off to dangle about her wrist. Everett jerked down her hands and the bag slipped to the floor, its contents scattering everywhere like spent cartridges after a bloody battle.

Flinging him off, blinking furiously to keep back the

tears that weren't remotely connected to the spilled purse, she dropped to her knees on the floor.

"Look what you've done!" she cried.

Everett didn't give the first glance at the clutter on the floor. He gazed down at the tears that brimmed and finally spilled in drizzling, diamond arcs over her cheeks. Tooth prints were engraved in her lower lip, where they'd nearly drawn blood.

He despised himself and felt the condemnation of a crime he wasn't aware of committing. Lowering a knee beside hers, he braced back on his heel. He cupped the side of her jaw and tenderly tipped up her face.

"I am looking, sweetheart," he said huskily, wiping the tears with both his thumbs. "And I swear I don't know what to do with what I see."

She couldn't, Jenny told herself, follow her instincts to fling herself into his arms. In a voice as controlled as she could make it, she wept, "You can't walk in here and buy my understanding with bribes, Everett. You . . ." Her shoulders shook as she remembered the unbelievably tender things they had done and said those nights in Spain. "You just can't do that."

"No one's bribing anyone."

"Yes, you are! You call up Pamela Chase and tell her some firm of Wells and Associates—"

"It *is* Wells and Associates."

She began blotting her face on the sleeve of her jacket. "You know what I'm talking about."

"You're the one we want to do the job. That has absolutely nothing to do with bribes."

"You bought my house!"

"Oh." Everett nibbled at the edge of his lip, having hoped they could deal with that later. "I see you found out about that."

"Found out? *Found out?*" She found a Kleenex that had spilled on the floor and wiped her nose with it.

"Why? That's what I'd like to know. When Esther Simmons told me, I thought you'd decided to put the research complex on Ferris Street. Then I would have at least lost to something worthwhile. But now, seeing this . . ." Jenny indicated the walls around them. "Explain it to me, Everett. Why did you buy my house if it isn't a bribe?"

Everett pretended to examine the walls she spoke of. The ache in his stomach was killing him. How cutting her scorn was! "You're pretty good at figuring things out, Ms. Howard. You tell me."

"Then give me credit," she said with determined effort, "for figuring out a few other things too."

"Like Ruth?"

"I don't want to talk about her."

"I'll bet you don't."

She began gathering up her spilled purse.

Everett grabbed her hands and positioned himself over her until he was practically straddling her legs. He lowered their hands to her knees and kept his clasped firmly about hers. She refused to look up, but he thought that was just as well.

"It was nothing, Jenny," he admitted softly while he could still get the words out. Leaning forward, he let his forehead rest upon hers. His words fell upon the curves of her face.

"What you saw was nothing, sweetheart. I tried to explain to you the things Ruth was capable of. She'd come there to sell out. We'd been up half the night trying to reach an agreement. When she got up to go to the bathroom, the next thing I knew, you were there. She walked out like . . . that. I've seen her do so many imbecilic things, I didn't realize for a moment that you could possibly take it seriously. Then you . . . were gone."

Jenny took it all in. She began inching backward so that he wasn't touching her. When she began to shiver, he reached out, but she shook her head in a warning to not touch her. "Why didn't you say something before I left?"

"Because you stood there with that horror all over your face, condemning me on circumstantial evidence."

"But you could have come after me. I would've believed you."

"Pride?" Everett spread his wide, browned hands upon his knees. "Ego? Who knows why fools do what they do? After what we'd had in Talencia, I couldn't believe you'd really think I was capable of something that underhanded. Ruth and I had a terrible quarrel. Which ended, incidentally, in my having to pay her a good deal more than she'd agreed to. Later, so much time elapsed it was like you were putting the screws to me, wanting me to . . ." He gave her his profile. ". . . to beg, or something."

"Talk about misjudging people."

"Well, at least demanding an apology from me for something I didn't do."

Jenny looked at the top of his head when it bent with a longing beyond all her comprehension. She was at his mercy, simply because she did believe him. But he mustn't know. She was lost if he knew.

"Oh, Lord," he breathed, then lifted his gaze to hers. "I shouldn't have waited so long to tell you this."

Thinking she might survive if she could just get out of this room and digest all this, Jenny began crawling about to scoop up her compact and her wallet and her brush and car keys. She kept her face averted so he couldn't discover her vulnerability.

"I'm really pressed for time, Everett. I—"

Everett had picked up her lipstick, which had rolled beside his foot. Pulling off the cap, he drew it beneath his nose like a bottle of heady perfume.

"You were wearing this when I kissed you on the back porch that day."

Her face was a mixture of astonishment and mistrust when she lifted it.

He grinned and let the hesitation speak for itself. Softly he said, "Seconds on the kiss, darling?"

An electric shock riveted through Jenny, making her want to curl herself into a knot and become invisible. She caught her balance with her fingertips on the floor and reddened until her skin burned.

"Why do you do that, Jenny?"

"You have no mercy," she mumbled.

"Why, because I like the way you taste? I could taste you . . ." He toyed with the word until it became unbearably erotic.

Her cheeks continued to flame, her throat, her arms.

". . . all night long," he finished thickly.

"Give me that!" She snatched at the lipstick in a blistering memory of him doing just that.

But Everett held it over her head, beyond her reach. He replaced the cap and dropped the tube into the pocket of his jacket.

"I can get another," she said with an aloofness that wasn't at all what she felt.

She pushed herself up from the floor. She was hardly aware of herself walking to the door and placing her hand upon the glass knob. Everett was very close behind her as she paused. Only inches separated them.

Impulsively, for he didn't know if she would allow him to touch her or not, Everett slipped an arm about her right shoulder. When she didn't try to pull away, he closed it to form a cautious loop about her neck. Carefully he lowered his lips to the nape of her neck.

"Oh, Jenny," he breathed against the smooth, silky span. "Oh, Jenny."

She was trembling in his arms. He could almost feel the blood moving through her body. Emboldened, he strained very close until she was trapped between the door and the length of his body. He pressed even nearer until his bones imbedded themselves into the swell of her hips.

"I go to sleep seeing your face in my mind," he muttered against the shell of her ear. He blew delicately, thrilling at the shiver that traveled up her back. "Your name is on the tip of my tongue when I wake up. Can you get someone else who wants you like I do, Jenny? Can you search the world and find someone who needs you like I do?"

He let one hand slide casually over her ribs and gradually spread his fingers wide. With the tip of his thumb he began stroking the lowest curve of her breast. "Can you find someone who wants to make you happy for the rest of his life?"

As if someone had swiveled her by the hair of the head, Jenny turned in his arms. Her eyes came into focus, and she saw the panic lurking deep in the blue of Everett's—a haunted truth that he couldn't entirely disguise, even though he was trying. She could guess how much it cost him to say such a thing. He wasn't touching her now, and she slipped away from him, shaking her head exactly as he had earlier.

"Oh, you do have a way about you, Everett Black," she said breathlessly. "I'll give you that."

The silence was all around them, stemming from a history that had detoured far around their youth and had now traced its way back. Suddenly the quiet was welcome. They let the minutes bathe them like gentle rain after weeks of brutal drought. They stood without any thoughts of blame or censure and realized that they were facing each other after a dreadful, prolonged wounding. Yet, they were still who they were, slightly battered but intact, together in this place, understanding more than before.

After a time she said in a small, thin voice, "But I don't know where to go from here."

His smile was relief and elation. He reached out a hand and brushed the curls back from her face, and she saw they were unsteady.

"We don't go anywhere," he said. "I truly didn't come here to hurt you, Jenny. I came to get a job done and you're the one I wanted. About . . . what I said just now, I meant it, and I know it won't be easy to work out. Let's just . . ."

For the first time today she smiled. It occurred to her that it was the first time she'd truly smiled since she'd come home. "Just let nature take its course?" she prompted shyly.

He touched one of her dimples and grinned. "It's worked for a long time, my lady."

She let her lips curve pleasantly upward. "Spain taught us both a few things," she said, for she still had her one dark truth about Ruth tucked away deep in her heart.

"Then let's let things cool off. Walk with me. Let me introduce you to some of the people you'll be working with if you take the job. I'm not conning you when I say it would be a fun project. And it'd look pretty good in your bank account too." He chuckled. "Besides, Dave is here. He wants to see you."

Dave's rousing bear hug caught Jenny by surprise. Not that she didn't enjoy being swept up in his arms and hugged until her ribs nearly cracked. His warmth was like this day, unseasonable and vastly pleasant. It was the memory of Ruth that the sight of him triggered, that and the knowledge that within her lay the power to change Everett in ways he didn't dream possible. Would he change for good or for bad? That was the trouble with tiny deceptions: Once they were shuffled around from postponement to postponement, they were suddenly no longer tiny.

She felt dizzy when Dave set her upon her feet.

"My, but you're a sight for my eyes!" he razzed her, because she was blushing. "If Everett weren't my best friend, I'd steal you for myself."

When she stuck out her tongue and laughed at him, he clasped her frilly head between his big hands and grinned down at her. "Aw, I don't know, Everett," he drawled with mock sobriety. "Seems to me braces wouldn't have helped that much."

"Oh, you!" she scolded. "I'm very sensitive about my teeth, I'll have you know. And I don't take kindly to being ribbed about them."

Dave looked over his shoulder at Everett, who stood, hands in his pockets, enjoying every minute of it. "And you said she'd forgive you anything," he said.

"I've been conspired against," she yelped, and let them each loop one of her arms in theirs. They looked as if they were in a parade. When she realized that they were passing messages over her head with their glances, she grasped a wisp of hair on the back of Everett's hand and tweaked it until he yelled.

"Ouch! You little brawler! What'd I do now?"

"It's impolite to talk about someone when they're not there to defend themselves," she retorted. "You should look out for my best interests."

Feeling better than he'd felt in weeks, Everett placed a firm swat on the side of her hip. She jumped, and her brows blunted together.

"Mothers look out for your best interests," he said.

"And sisters who were too young to remember how mean you were at twelve. Speaking of which, I told my mother I was bringing you by to see her."

Before Jenny could digest the significance of his taking such a step, to say nothing of the fact that he'd made this arrangement before their confrontation today, Everett signaled someone with a wave of his arm.

"Coming," he yelled in the direction of the slab. "Take care of her, Dave. I'll be right back."

Together they watched Everett saunter off with that sexy, Richard Gere stroll of his. Jenny stood with her arm still looped through Dave's.

Amazed, she said, "Do you know that's the first time he's ever wanted me to see his mother?"

Dave squinted into the sunlight at the slab. He smelled like Doublemint chewing gum.

For lack of anything better to do, they'd begun ambling toward the small copse of pine trees farther from the group of conversing men. The sky was cool and serene, not preparing her at all for Dave's words. They hit her like an unseen blow to the back of her head.

"Jennifer," he peered down at her in his abrupt, straightforward manner, "Everett damn near went to pieces when you left Spain."

Not only was this announcement a breathtaking shock, she didn't know where it would lead. She stood plucking at the ribbing of her sweater. Her voice was as thin as tissue. "What do you mean, went to pieces?"

"I mean, he got a bottle and dug in for three days and nights. Wouldn't let anyone come near him except me, and I couldn't get anything out of him except a bunch of vicious talk that he didn't know he was saying."

She placed her case carefully beside her feet, as if it

contained nitroglycerin, as if she could be destroyed by the slightest breath.

"I don't think we should be saying these things," she said tightly, dismayed at the trembling of her knees.

Dave mistook her irritation as being meant for him. "Why not?" he bristled. "We both love him. Doesn't that count for something?"

"But I—" She drew back, her eyes wide with unbearable images of Everett grieving.

"You can't deny it, Jennifer. You love him as much as I do. It's as inseparable from you as the very air you breathe. A lot of vitally important things depend upon Everett, do you realize that? If he goes down, a lot of lives that might have been saved go down the tubes with him. I could protect him from Ruth because he didn't have any hang-ups about her. But you? How can I protect him from his own heart?"

Both of them automatically looked out where Everett conversed with the contractors. He was shading his eyes from the sun with one hand as he swept his other arm out to encompass the entirety of the land. His clothes moved with him as his legs flexed and swiveled. He was so utterly magnificent with the sunlight glinting off his hair. Knowing that he cared enough about the condition of the world to be doing this, Jenny felt a low, deep wrenching that was almost unbearable. How she loved this man! How she wanted to remember him exactly this way!

"If I didn't think you were the only one who could get him back on a level keel," Dave was saying quietly, "I wouldn't be telling you this. He won't let me get inside him on this. I can't reach him."

Though some of what he'd said made her feel invaded, Jenny met his gaze with understanding. "We don't mean to hurt each other."

"Love never does."

"And it's never that simple. There are still a few things, Dave, to be healed."

Dave slipped a piece of chewing gum from his pocket and began unpeeling it. He crushed the paper into a tiny sphere, wound up, and threw it at the sun.

"Give him a little time, that's all, that's all I'm asking you. Just . . ." He spread out his hands. "Give him a little time."

Jenny felt herself tumbling into the depths of Dave's very large compassion. From the slab Everett motioned for her to meet him at the parking lot. Suddenly, impulsively, she stood on tiptoe and kissed his cheek.

"I like you, Dave Lytton," she said.

He grinned down at her. "And I like you. Don't be afraid to take a chance, Jenny. In the words of the immortal Rocky Balboa . . ."

Together they chimed in, *"Go for it!"*

Laughing, she hugged herself. Everett was waiting for her, one hand threading through his shining black hair. "You say that to the original jellyfish," she said.

He touched her chin with a mock fist. "I don't think so."

When she glanced back, Dave was unpeeling another piece of chewing gum and walking toward the cement slab.

"What did you talk about?" was the first thing Everett asked when they matched their steps. Their shadows skittered crazily across the asphalt.

"Fools," she answered with hesitation.

He flicked her a curious glance. "Which one, you or me?"

"The biggest one," she said cryptically, wondering now if she would ever find a way to tell him Ruth's lie. Perhaps it would only send him back into another reversal as cruel as the one he'd just suffered.

"Did you really tell your mother that you were bringing me to see her?" she asked, trying to push the prickings of her conscience aside.

"Shouldn't I have?"

She laughed. "It's all right. How are you going to face the ordeal of *my* mother?"

He pulled a tragic grief across his face, stiffened his back, then held up an imaginary pince-nez and fitted it. "Ach! You are not to vorry. I haff a way, my dahlink. Leef it to me."

Giggling, she said, "I think you'd better tell me. Any more surprises, and I don't promise what will happen."

He dropped the pince-nez into the pocket of his jacket. "In that case, let's go look at it."

Chapter Eleven

$\mathscr{P}$erhaps it was the freshness of the day. Or the exhilaration of the sunshine. Or Everett's earnestness when he said again that he loved her. Jenny thought the old house on Ferris Street had a decidedly improved look about it. The windows, instead of appearing like haunted, disappointed eyes, seemed to blink in the sunshine, as if they were waking up like Rip van Winkle after an aging sleep.

"Look, Everett!" she cried happily. She moved ahead of him, stooping gracefully and lifting the tender branches of the willow that swept the ground. "See? It's beginning to bud. Spring is almost here."

Smiling, she tossed the branches into the air like confetti. They fell artlessly to the ground.

She was so lovely and winsome, Everett thought. So totally unlike Ruth. He could have stood there for hours, watching her. All the misgivings and worry he'd suffered in Spain burned away like the dew on the grass at his feet. He wanted her. Whatever price it would cost to get her and to hold her forever, he would gladly pay it.

Jenny skittered up the steps to the house and cupped her hand upon the stained glass of the door. She peered inside as if she could actually see.

"Here," he said a little huskily, wanting to touch her but not daring to break the spell. "This belongs to you. I think you should do the honors."

Turning back, she saw the key to the house. It dangled from his fingers by a chain. Not understanding, she sought his eyes, lips half-smiling. "But—"

"The house is yours, sweetheart," he explained. "Here, take the key. Open the door."

The color drained from her face. The smile faded, and her shoulders drooped. "Mine?" she breathed in astonishment.

"Yours."

"But you . . . I . . ."

Everett slipped the key in the lock, turned it, and pushed open the door. Then he unzipped the handbag draping over her shoulder and dropped the key into it. "*Your* house, Jenny. No strings. Free and clear."

The fulfillment of her dream? The Prince Charming kissing the Sleeping Beauty and awakening her to a new life? Impossible! She shook her head.

"You don't understand," she mumbled, following him inside. When had he bought the house? Before Spain? The day they'd kissed?

"I understand perfectly."

The interior was dim with shadows. Though Jenny knew there was no electricity, she automatically flipped the light switch on, then off. She was numbly reliving the day Esther Simmons had thought she and Everett were married and had shown them the house. Another lifetime ago.

"Well?" Everett said briskly, turning in a circle after he stepped into the living room. "What will you remodel first? Upstairs? Downstairs? The antique shop? I suppose you'll make almost all the lower floor the shop, won't you? That and Mildred's rooms?"

Jenny was still in a state of disbelief. "I don't believe this."

He seemed absorbed in inspecting the fireplace. She stepped behind him and watched him shift one of the andirons with the toe of his shoe. Soot filtered down from the chimney and he replaced the screen.

"Everett," she began haltingly, touching his sleeve, then drawing back.

He turned.

She hardly knew what to say. "First of all"—she lifted one palm—"I want you to know that I'm over-whelmed you would want to give me—give the boys, too, and Mother—this wonderful gift. But don't you see? I can't accept . . ." She threw out her hand out to include the high ceiling and walls. ". . . this."

Everett rested both elbows upon the mantel and leaned backward. His jacket fell open to reveal his leanness, the deceptive discipline of his body. He averted his head enough so that he could stroke his upper lip and therefore not look at her. "Why not?"

"Because . . . because . . ." she sputtered, "it's just not done. That's why not."

"Because I once forfeited the right?"

"You know better than that. Give me a gift if you must. I'd adore one—flowers, a tennis racket, any-thing. But not a house!"

In one fluid movement he came away from the mantel, as if he had suddenly spied a curl out of place on the side of her head. He casually rearranged it, bent back from his waist to survey whether or not he liked it that way, all without looking at her eyes or responding to her reaction.

"Everett!"

Still fussing over the errant curl, he said calmly, "Why can't a husband give his wife a house if he wants to?"

Her desire to hear those words had been a part of her growing up for so long, a part of her pain of living, that her disbelief made her draw back. She leaned far away from him, her eyes wide, her lips parted, as if she were seeing him for the very first time.

He grinned crookedly. "I'm not certain I should be flattered by your reaction to my proposal of marriage, my sweet. Maybe I should say it another way."

"No!" She blinked hard. "No other way. I—" In spite of everything she could do, huge, solemn tears filled her eyes. They clung precariously to her lashes, then spilled down her cheeks, running into the places where her dimples were and coursing down her chin.

At a loss, feeling almost as if he were drowning in those spilled tears, Everett stood curling his fingers into impotent fists. "I didn't mean to make you cry," he said with grating honesty.

Her eyes widened even more. "Am I crying?"

Smiling, shaking his head, he took her into his arms and cushioned her cheek against his shoulder. "If it were anyone else, I'd say yes. With you I'm not sure."

For the first time in weeks, maybe in her whole life, Jenny felt perfectly safe. She snuggled against his shoulder. *Now,* a voice whispered in her head. *Now is the time. Tell him what Ruth has done.* But she'd waited too many years for this moment. How could she risk something—anything—that would mar the perfection of it? *Later,* she told the voice. *There is time enough.*

Everett let his fingers trail over the subtle bones of

her back. "Am I supposed to take your silence as a yes or a no?"

Without warning Jenny tipped up her head. The smile that shone through her tears was as startling as a rainbow. "Come," she said, and darted through the door toward the stairs. Her footsteps flew, followed by the heavier, more uncertain tread of Everett's. She flung open a door that faced the front of the house: the bedroom where she'd turned from a girl into a woman, the room where she'd faced the tragedy of losing him and picking up the pieces of her life.

Feeling slightly in awe, she walked across the room and peered out of the window. Her tears were drying upon her cheeks, and she reached behind herself, knowing Everett was there.

Everett placed his hand in hers and stepped firmly into her back. His chin came to the top of her curls, and he nestled it upon the crown of her head. When he wrapped his arms about her, she snuggled back and let out her breath as if she had come an enormously long distance to get to this place.

"Do you remember?" She gazed down at the ruffled willow branches that the breeze lifted like streamers of green lace. "Do you remember all the things we said beneath that tree?"

"My memories," he answered, burying his face into the fragrance of her curls, "keep getting mixed up. Right now I'm remembering a lady in Barcelona who told me about Bizet and frightened me because of the things she made me see about myself."

She listened to his breathing, which came too fast, and enjoyed the way he tried to stand without moving when he wanted to cover her with kisses.

"Do our scars run too deep, Everett?" she asked with stunning solemnity. "Are we both fools for standing here with the word *marriage* dangling between us?"

For a time he didn't reply. "I don't know. Yes, I do know. Well, I know we're not fools."

"Does it scare you to think about our history?"

"Yes. Does it scare you?"

She took a deep breath. "One thing scares me more."

"What?"

She turned in his arms with utmost care. "Living without you."

Standing there, the sunshine bursting golden at her back, Everett thought she looked like an angel. He touched her lips with his fingers. Slowly they traveled upward, over the bones of her cheeks, the curve of her forehead. His thumbs traced the span of her brows.

"All those years when I was alone, I would've given everything I had to hear those words," he said.

Her head bent slightly with the weight of the past. "And whenever I look back . . . Oh, Everett, what do we do with the years? All the years?"

It was as if his proposal had spread out their lives like a hand of cards for them to see. "We can't do anything but accept them as they are," he said. "Nothing's ever wasted, not if you don't want it to be. All the pain, all the years—they make us what we are."

"And what are we?"

"Two people who have loved. And lost. And survived the years. Two people whom time has touched and who love more because of it."

"Then it's not wrong to say"—she paused to search for the right words—"to say that I love you more than I ever could have before?"

He smiled. "There's something to be said for losing and finding. Remember the prodigal son? Are you going to say yes to my proposal of marriage, Jenny, or do I give you this ring anyway?"

It was a shock, something she'd never expected.

Jenny stood unmoving as he drew the ring from his pocket, hardly able to think except to see that his fingers were as shaky as hers when he placed the ring upon her finger.

"What?" she said dumbly, staring at it.

"No, darling. Repeat after me: Yes, Everett, I love you and I'll marry you."

She laughed breathlessly. "Yes, yes, yes, yes!"

Coming to life, she threw her arms about his chest. Instinctively he sought the comfort of her breast, and she let him. She covered the hard brown hand with her own as if she would keep it there forever.

"Where would we live?" she said, snuggling against him. "In Boston? Here? You're such an important man, my darling. Would you drag us around the world if I married you?"

His laughter rumbled. "My office is where I am, but your work is here. I don't want your life disrupted, or the boys'. Kiss me, Jenny."

Her musing drifted contentedly. "Would we have a regular wedding?" Her head came up. "You mean you'd go through that, Everett—the church and the ceremony and everything?"

The dimples in her cheeks flashed so adorably, he kissed one. "Dave can give away the bride." Then the other dimple. "Jeffrey can be my best man." His mouth was working its way over her face. "We'd have two mothers, if no fathers. Kiss me, Jenny."

Jenny's breath fluttered out of control. Sparkling tingles attacked her legs and made her head float as if it weren't hers at all. He was hard and wanting against her waist—pressing, urging.

"You mean," she said, dodging his amorous caresses, "I would have it all? The wedding, the house, my family? Mother's shop? Everything?"

"Kiss me, Jenny," he groaned, and bent over her.

"Pamela could be my maid of honor," she managed to choke out before he crushed her.

"Anything. Stop talking before I go mad."

She stood on the tips of her toes and met his burning lips. "We can't have anyone going mad," she said, but that was all, for neither of them said anything after that.

After a time Everett glanced around them, not particularly pleased with his options. The empty room wasn't the most convenient place for a tryst. "Do you know how much I want you at this moment?"

It wasn't that Jenny didn't burn from the same pent-up fires as he did. Yet, a morality that had been instilled when she was a child, the same morality that had pained her when they'd made love before, now confronted her mercilessly. She leaned back in his arms.

"Please," she shook her head, "let's wait."

His confusion flickered across his face. "But before—"

She hushed him with fingertips upon his lips. He kissed them. "I know. And I've paid a price for that, too, Everett. Please, let's play by the rules from now on. Couldn't we start life all over again, from this very moment? Like we were brand new?"

Everett drew himself up so tall he appeared to tower above her. "We aren't new, darling."

"I know. But I want to be a bride for you, Everett. Just like when I was a girl. I want to wait and savor it and go to sleep wanting you so badly I could die."

Smiling because he loved her—and, in a disjointed, haphazard way, even seeing the sense in what she said, Everett held her at arm's length and laughed. "Name the date, then. But for God's sake, don't make it long. Not unless you want me ruined for life."

She answered without hesitation. "The first day of spring. Late in the evening, when everything is so beautiful."

He lowered his lips to hers, not in burning passion now, but in gentle respect for the vast distance they had traveled to meet each other. "*You* are beautiful. And I ask only one thing of you."

She gazed up with trusting eyes. "What?"

"Make the house fit," he said. "Do what you will to it so we can start our life together from this place. Just you and me."

She truly was beautiful when she smiled. "You and me and the willow tree."

"I love you," he said, and kissed her again.

The days were a whirl—deliriously happy, mad with activity. Everett spent every free moment with her family, coming to know the boys, wearing down Mildred's conditioned resistance, returning to the Bentley Hotel only when Jenny forcibly evicted him.

"I expect to see him with his suitcase any day now," Mildred said at the breakfast table. "He might as well move in. He lives over here."

Jenny laughed. Her mother was mellowing wonderfully. She had even telephoned Everett's mother and made a date for lunch.

"I wish he would," Jeffrey said with his mouth full. He was avidly devouring a book propped on the milk carton. "He explained the Federal Reserve System to me."

"How many times have I told you it's rude to read at the table?" his grandmother scolded.

Jeffrey looked at his book as if it were a small fortune in gold. "But this is calculus, Grandma. I need to know it if I'm going to Ellison's next year."

Mildred closed the book and gazed over her coffee

cup. "And that's another thing. How will you get to Ellison's? Do you know it's halfway into Atlanta?"

Jeffrey slipped the book between his back and the chair. "Everett said he'd take care of all that."

Stephen glanced up from his cereal. His happy smile beamed. "He can, too. Everett can do anything."

Mildred hid her smile behind a cough. "Not quite, Stephen. Finish your breakfast. And you, Jeffrey, you still have this year to finish with Mr. Prescott at middle school. Don't get too big for your britches."

Jeffrey grinned. "Mr. Prescott said he'll be glad to be rid of me."

Laughing, for she had already received the principal's wholehearted approval for Jeffrey's change of school, Jenny scraped back her chair. "I hate to leave you all, but this is the last day to get the furniture for the master bedroom and the rest of the kitchen done. Everett is so fussy. It'll take months to finish the downstairs like he wants it."

Mildred, too, pushed back from the table. "I'm supposed to meet him today and go over plans for the antique shop. I hate to go over there. There're are so many people working on that house already, you can hardly find standing room. It doesn't feel like you'll be getting married tomorrow."

"Well, I am." Placing a quick kiss on her mother's cheek, grabbing up the jacket to her smart J & H slack suit, Jenny flipped through the previous day's mail on her way out the door. "I'll see you then. By the way, the telephones are working now. It was quite elaborate, what with keeping your apartment and the shop separated from the rest of the house. Call me."

Mildred flushed slightly. "Everett's gone far out of his way to see that I'll have my own things. I could stay here, you know, in this house. And I wouldn't mind. Honestly."

Jenny tossed the mail aside and hugged her mother. "Do you think we'd allow that? Why, what would the boys do without you to keep them in line?"

"Yeah, Grandma," Stephen chimed in. "You've been griping at me ever since I can remember."

Fondly tweaking his ear, Mildred said, "I never gripe, youngster. I advise but I never gripe."

The boys laughed and bustled about getting things ready for school. Jenny shook her head. "Everett would never hear of your living somewhere else, Mother, and neither would I. It's a large house."

Busying herself quite suddenly with clearing the table, Mildred didn't reply. As she pushed against the door to the kitchen, she chokingly cleared her throat.

Jenny met the eyes of her older son. Jeffrey winked at her with approval and she sighed contentedly. Jeffrey's haunted frustration had almost disappeared, ever since she'd told him that she was going to marry Everett. He was settling at last, she thought.

"You boys behave," she called out. "I have to go now."

They hurled the usual vague promises at her back as she walked through the door.

Jenny didn't know where the morning went. She worked through lunch, which was a mistake with the hectic pace of the last days. An attack of dizziness virtually overcame her. The moment the furniture store delivered the king-size bed and set it up, she stretched out to rest. She'd better order something to eat, too, she warned herself, or she wouldn't be able to make it to her own wedding.

After a sandwich and a glass of milk she felt almost human again. Last-minute arrangements about the wedding consumed over an hour. It was to be a simple affair at St. Christopher's. Only the family would attend, and a few very dear friends. The cream-colored silk suit and a wide-brimmed hat had already been delivered. The rector, an old family friend who'd insisted that the two families be his guests in the parish house after the ceremony, was handling everything himself. Things were running without a flaw, except for Pamela, who vowed and declared that Jenny was making the worst mistake of her life by getting married again.

The afternoon was perfect for the last day of her single life, Jenny thought as she ambled through the downstairs. The house was thrown wide for the window washers and smelled marvelously fresh and clean. The painters had finished with the exterior, and the downstairs was nearly completed, as much as could be done in the short time allotted her.

Pleasantly tired, she stood in the open doorway, breathing in the welcome fragrance of daffodils and lilacs. She was so absorbed in her daydreams that she hardly saw the Seville when it drew up to the curb and slammed one of its doors. Bartlett Street gave her an elegant bow as he strode extravagantly up the sidewalk.

"I had to stop and see," he called, removing a foppish hat as he came up the walk. "You're a clever vixen, Mrs. Howard. You bought it out from under me. I was going to put a curved display window precisely where you're standing."

Laughing, Jenny went to meet him. "I did nothing of the sort. Someone bought it out from under me, and I had to promise to marry him to get it back."

Bartlett held her arms, his eyebrows working with mock sternness. "Why, I would have made that arrangement myself if I'd known that was all it would take."

"I'm afraid it was slightly more complicated, Mr. Street." Letting him loop her arm through his, Jenny walked back toward the freshly painted porch.

He patted her hand. "Knowing you, my dear, I'm sure it was. You're looking unusually beautiful today."

"Why, thank you. Did you know that anyone who says that wins a free tour through the house?"

He chuckled. "I was counting on it."

Though she'd never considered Bartlett Street to be one of her favorite people, Jenny nonetheless found him to be absolutely charming. He listened to her plans about the antique shop, all her ramblings about Everett's work, and the wonderful things he was doing for the world.

"I've always wanted to do something for mankind," he said with enthusiastic self-criticism. "I was so busy making property settlements with my ex-wives that I never found time for it. Such a tragedy."

"See how lucky I am, then," she laughed. "Being poor does have its advantages. Let me show you what we're planning for the upstairs."

Everett was thankful that Dave had come with him when he drove Mildred across town to Ferris Street. He wasn't sure that he'd ever get over his feeling of chagrin when Jenny's mother leveled at him eyes that remembered every dumb thing he'd ever done.

"It's going to be a great spring," he said gruffly when he parked his car behind the Seville.

Mildred found herself rather enjoying this handsome, sophisticated man's awkwardness. "Yes," she said. "Your mother's a lovely woman, Everett. We had a nice lunch today."

"Thank you." Everett coughed lightly into his hand.

"Here, Mrs. Stephenson," offered Dave, tactfully hacking through the tension, "let me help you out."

"I can do it myself," she protested proudly. "I'm not an old woman."

Dave chuckled. "Well, then, would you mind helping me out?"

They laughed, and Everett sent his old friend a silent thank-you over Mildred's head. Relaxing somewhat, the three of them browsed about the porch, commenting on the vast amount of work that had been accomplished, inspecting the window washers at their work, then climbing the steps.

Jenny didn't even hear the three of them as she and Bartlett descended the stairs. Bartlett paused to study the circular stained-glass window halfway down and tried to place the period. When he stopped abruptly in her path, Jenny stumbled into him.

"Oh!" she said, and bent forward, catching her face in her hands.

"Oh, my dear," Bartlett murmured sympathetically. "Here, let me—"

Jenny waved him away. "No, no." Her eyes closed, for she felt her head swimming off somewhere in space. Inching to the banister, she draped over it. Nausea swam up into her throat, and she clapped her hand over her mouth, remaining perfectly still and praying everything would stay down.

"Are you all right?" Bartlett asked in a moment, taking her by the shoulders when she finally settled enough to lift her head. "You're as pale as death."

"Ah . . . just a little . . ." She dragged her fingers through her curls and stood holding the back of her neck.

"A little afternoon sickness?" he chuckled. "Hmm, little mother-to-be?"

The truth had a feel to it when Bartlett Street put it into words, a ruthlessness that seemed to draw a pall over the sunshine of the afternoon. What amazed Jenny was that she hadn't guessed before now: The monthly cycle that wasn't quite right and the second one that had never come.

"I—" She couldn't even get out her words as her mind raced through the signs she should have seen. "I guess . . . so."

"Well"—Bartlett gave her hand a fatherly pat—"I'm sure of it. I didn't go through all my wives without learning a few things, my dear. Congratulations. You must have a daughter now, after two strapping sons."

The movement at the bottom of the stairway was little more than a hazy impression. When Jenny gaped down at Everett's stunned face, aware of the shock of Dave and her mother, she felt a large, gaping hole blow through her. All her life seemed to scatter about her in bits and pieces. She was in Everett's mind, reading the truth as surely as he had read hers when she'd watched Ruth walk out of that office in Spain. *You're having a baby?* she heard his thoughts shouting at her. *Whose baby?*

"Ah," said Bartlett Street, having no idea of the damage that had been done, "and this must be the groom." He stepped lightly down the stairs and looked back at Jenny. "Introduce me, my dear."

For the rest of her life Jenny would wonder how she ever got through the next two minutes. "Mr. Street," she said in a voice that came by some mechanical process she was ignorant of, "I'd like you to meet Everett Black, my fiancé."

She wasn't certain if Everett replied or not. She saw the men shake hands, and she saw her mother look at her with dumbfounded horror. She tried to catch Everett's eyes, praying for some miracle of understanding, some sliver of hope that she could go on with this. He refused to look at her.

Leave, then! her mind shrieked to him. *Believe that of*

me if you can! Was this, then, the payment for her indiscretion of stolen moments in his arms?

"Jenny?" Dave jumped to the emergency that his intuition warned him was critical. "I was to give you a message," he lied flagrantly. "You're supposed to return a phone call immediately. So nice meeting you, Mr. Street. Would you excuse us a moment?"

Before anyone could object, certainly before Everett could even get his bearings, Dave whisked Jenny out of the hall and rushed her to the rear of the house. "Where's the kitchen?"

She waved her hand in the general direction, and he steered her through a door and grabbed the first chair he found.

"Sit down," he commanded.

She obeyed without protest.

Finding a cupboard, he ran some tap water in a glass and held it in front of her face. "Drink it."

"Did you see Everett?" she choked, and grabbed his wrist, sending water sloshing over her lap.

Dave grabbed a towel and began wiping across her lap as if she were a child. "Yes," he said, "I saw. I don't understand, but I saw."

"Oh, Dave." She buried her face in her hands.

"Jenny, you can't go to pieces now. Listen to me."

"I didn't know I was pregnant. I swear."

"That doesn't matter now. The first thing you're going to do is get Everett in here and get this thing out in the open."

Her head snapped up, ravaged. "You think it's not his?" Her eyes flared wetly.

Dave was uncertain of how to answer her. "Well," he hesitated, "I mean, I know that he's—"

"He's nothing. It was Ruth all those years, Dave. She tricked him into thinking he couldn't have children. She told me. I meant to tell him, and I—"

Feeling somewhat dazed, Daved pulled her up from the chair and folded her in his arms. "Shh," he soothed her, his mind whirling. "Everything'll be all right. Shh, you'll make yourself sick."

"I'm already sick," she wailed. "Did you see his face?"

"I'll talk to him," he promised her. "Don't worry about anything. I'll—"

"No!" Jenny jerked away from him. She couldn't beg Everett to believe her, not after the glittering accusation she'd read in his eyes. She rubbed her own eyes and mumbled behind her hands. "I appreciate what you're trying to do, Dave. But no, I have to work this out for myself. After what I saw in there, I'm not sure I can. But please . . ."

Dave suffered premonitions of disaster. "Don't do something stupid, Jennifer. You'll regret it."

"What's one more regret?"

"Jenny?" Mildred opened the door. "May I come in?"

Jenny held her breath, expecting Everett to follow her mother into the room. But no one came through the door. No footsteps sounded, no hurt face confronted hers so she could look at it with love and say she would explain everything.

Looking about himself, suddenly feeling in the way, Dave cleared his throat. "Well, I think I'll just run along, Jenny. I won't do anything if you tell me not to, but please, follow some very old, very good advice. Don't let the sun set on your anger."

Over her head Mildred and Dave exchanged a saddened, wordless message. They shook their heads.

Jenny could hardly look at Dave when he left. Her body was making too many demands, and the exhaustion threatened to overcome her. She needed to sleep, if only for a few minutes.

"You have to go to that man," Mildred said a half hour later, after she'd dragged the truth out of her daughter, one word at a time.

"I will. I swear I will." Jenny tried to stand up, and Mildred held her arm. "I just need to rest, Mother. For a few minutes. Please, go home and see that the boys get something to eat. I'll lie down here and get ahold of myself."

Suffering grave misgivings about leaving Jenny alone, Mildred walked with her to the master bedroom. She turned down the new bedspread and fluffed the pillows.

"Lie down," she ordered, guiding Jenny to the bed. "I should stay. You shouldn't be alone right now."

Jenny looked at the bed, the same one that had been delivered this afternoon, the same one she'd made up with new sheets and had daydreamed about: Everett and herself and the nights they would spend in it.

She shook her head. "I'll be all right," she said dully. Stooping, Mildred removed Jenny's shoes. When Jenny had stretched out, she smoothed the curls from off her forehead.

"Jenny," Mildred said with an urgency that made her voice quiver, "it's no secret how I've felt about Everett all these years. But I've been watching him since he's come back into our lives. He loves you, and he will love your sons. He loves them now because of you, but in the years to come they'll be like his own. That woman has done a terrible thing to him. Don't prolong his pain. Pick up the phone. He'll come to you."

"I know that." Jenny had her arm draped over her eyes. She couldn't bear to look at anything just now. "I'll call him, Mother. Just let me think about this new baby and what's happening to me."

The silence after Mildred left was a bottomless hole filled with voices that gave Jenny no peace. The miracle of her woman's body—that phenomenon that took control in order to protect itself—drugged her without mercy. Even now the tiny speck of life was making impossible demands upon her. *Rest,* it ordered. *Everything must come after me. Rest.* Heaven help her, what would happen to them all now?

The night before her daughter's wedding, Mildred sat alone in the dining room and wrestled with herself. The boys had gone to bed a half hour ago. Every ten minutes she had walked to the telephone, picked up the receiver, and replaced it. Now, thinking that meddling came in degrees and she was a most flagrant offender and didn't even care, she dialed the Bentley Hotel and asked for Dave Lytton.

"I sympathize, Mrs. Stephenson," Dave told her after Mildred had explained everything. "I really do. But a man has the right to his privacy, even a friend as close as Everett."

"She says she'll tell him, but you know how foolish people are when they're . . . in love. They're so proud. They're so . . . stupid."

Dave chuckled. "Yes, sad to say, I agree. But what you've just told me about Everett—that's a blow to any man. I'm not sure how he'll react."

Mildred pinched the bridge of her nose. "Just tell him."

By the time Dave knocked on Everett's door, only five down from his, Everett was coming to the door, buttoning on a fresh shirt. He had showered, and though he looked as if someone had battered his head, he did look better.

"You going out?" Dave looked at the uncharacteristic disorder of the room. Everett's clothes were flung everywhere and a half-consumed bottle of bourbon sat conspicuously on the table.

"A bachelor party?" Dave joked lamely.

"Yeah."

"Need some company?"

Everett shook his head.

"Everett—"

Everett held up his hand. "No, don't say it. I know I'm ten kinds of fool, but I've been sitting here thinking about it all evening. I don't give a damn what's happened or whose baby it is. I love her, and I'm going to marry her if she'll still have me. If that makes me a fool . . . well, dammit, it won't be the first time."

Giving a short laugh of disbelief, Dave walked to the bottle and tipped it up. He swigged off a large swallow, then coughed for a minute as the fire burned down his throat. He offered it to Everett, who shook his head. "Then take what I have to say standing up, my friend."

Everett blinked at him in confusion.

"It's your baby, Everett."

As if he'd been punched in the stomach, Everett bent slightly—winded, not believing it, but staggered. "Don't be gruesome. You know damn well—"

"I know what you *think* you know, my good friend. You think only what you've been told. Everett, Ruth conned you all those years. You can be a father just as easily as the next guy." He pulled a grimace. "Maybe a little easier than some, judging by how little you tried."

Rubbing his face, which had absolutely no color left at all, then wetting his lips, Everett walked straight to the bottle and tipped it back. He drained it nearly empty. For a moment he sat holding his head in his hands.

"There's been a mistake," he said.

"Ruth told Jennifer to her face. That was what the fuss was about in Spain. I'm sorry, old man, but you've been snookered by your ex-wife. It was a cruel, sick joke."

"Joke! It's been hell! A God-cursed, living hell!"

"Then don't make the wrong person pay!"

Everett strode to the closet and jerked open the door. It slammed against the wall with a crash that nearly ripped it off its hinges. He searched for a jacket and turned away with a curse.

Dave found his sport coat behind the chair. "Are you going to see her?"

"If she'll talk to me." Everett, still unable to believe everything that had happened to him in the space of hours, threaded his fingers through his hair. "I'll swear, Dave, I don't know what—"

"I know."

Stepping near the man who had saved him from a living death, Dave placed his hand on Everett's arm. Then, a bit desperately, he clasped his arms about him. For a moment they drew from the strengths of the other.

"It'll work out," Dave said gruffly, stepping back. "She loves you."

"I know." Everett wiped his hands across his eyes.

Chapter Twelve

$\mathcal{T}$he slender hands of the clock read a quarter to midnight when Jenny rose from the bed. From an old habit she began drifting through the house, shutting windows and drawing drapes. The mauve panels framing the dormer window of the living room whispered shut. For a moment she stood running her fingers over the luscious brocaded fabric. "It complements your hair," Everett had said when she'd showed him the sample. "Indulge me."

She bent double with the cruel burden of her memories. What was happening to her life?

Soundlessly she slipped through the darkness to the thermostat in the hall. She flipped on the light and tried to see the dial.

"Oh, damn!" she choked and let her forehead thump painfully upon the wall. "I never could read this miserable thing."

And that made her remember Everett waving the

opera tickets over her head and her silly attempts to read them. She could almost smell his after-shave when he'd bent his lips to hear her in the middle of all that deafening applause at the Gran Teatro Liceo. Sobs twisted painfully in her chest.

Finding her glasses, then not being able to see the thermostat through her blur of tears, she guessed at the setting and gave up. One by one she turned off the lights as she stumbled her way to the kitchen. Hardly anything sat on the newly painted shelves of the pantry. Tomorrow she must buy groceries, she thought, then covered her face with her hands. Tomorrow was her wedding day. Tomorrow was . . . tomorrow . . .

Somehow the sound of her own weeping comforted her. Sobbing hideously, she found club crackers and a box of tea. She filled the teakettle and put it on to boil. She cried until it boiled. With the tea brewed and everything put back in its place, she tiredly carried the tray to the bedroom. Sniffing, she considered calling her mother. Mildred would be worrying.

"Are you sure you'll be all right over there?" Mildred asked sleepily. "I don't like the thought of you being there all alone, Jenny."

"The doors are all locked, Mother. The heat's turned on. I'll be fine." She bit her lips, wanting dreadfully to ask if Everett had called. She couldn't bear to hear the word *no*. "I'll see you in the morning," she blurted quickly. "Cover for me with the boys."

"You know I will. Jenny, call him."

He hadn't called!

"I will," she whispered, agonized. Later, she thought, when she could bear the risk of seeing her life shatter in her hands.

Between sips of tea, Jenny undressed. Hiccoughing, she slipped into a long, belted robe. She hadn't even had the foresight to bring her gowns.

Feeling the tears crowding her head again, she cursed her own stupidity and wandered through the dark hall to the living room. Books and records were already on the shelves. How many hundreds of times had she slipped down the stairs in the dark to find a book in this room? She knew the way by memory.

Groping her way for a lamp, she sent a soft glow floating through the partially furnished room. The wallpaper still smelled fresh. The carpet was brand new and the sofa, an antique, was newly reupholstered in an elegant velour. It was a splendid, horribly empty room. Everything had been done for him!

Only a small collection of books had been moved in yet. The shelf shared its width with a half dozen demitasse cups and saucers. She wanted something by Graham Greene, she thought, even if she only read a few words. Clarity was what she needed tonight. Something sharp and spare.

But she couldn't see the titles. Tears kept spilling into her lashes.

"I suggest *War and Peace*," Everett said raggedly from the doorway. "The title's"—he paused to swallow—"quite fitting."

The demitasse cups and saucers went clattering to the floor as Jenny struck them with a startled forearm. She was already half kneeling. At the sound of his tortured voice, coupled with that of the crashing glass, she sank completely to the floor in shock. She didn't care how ugly she looked to him as she lifted her face distorted with her regret.

He was cradling her in his arms before she could say his name. She didn't fight it and she didn't ask why he was there. She only let herself go in the reassuring strength of his embrace.

"I know everything," he said.

"I was going to—"

"I didn't mean to—"

"A dozen times I tried . . ."

"Never again."

"It doesn't matter anymore."

She let Everett draw her into the hollow of his body until she didn't have a conception of either of them as separate entities. They were together again. The awful darkness was disappearing beneath the desperate assault of his mouth upon hers. Her lips clung with a searching entreaty, and his hands were everywhere, possessing the whole of her.

"Oh, Jenny," he moaned, "I didn't want to think about tomorrow without you."

"Forever was made for us," she whispered into his mouth. "Nothing will ever come between us."

He drew her out beneath him upon the carpet. Only days before, clad in jeans and old shirts, they'd huddled in the doorway and watched the men finish installing it. She had blushed at the outrageous things Everett said he would do to her before the fireplace on long winter nights. Now there was no fire except the one that drove Everett to part Jenny's robe and to take immense pleasure in the sight of her.

When he loved her, the taking wasn't so much an act of passion as it was the sealing of a commitment. When they were touching, as close as two people could touch each other, it truly struck him—the enormous fact of his child existing inside her. She was filled with him and with a part of them both that would go on and on. Everett cherished her with a tenderness beyond his own comprehension.

Later, when there were no more doubts of the future, Everett braced himself on an elbow and pulled her back against the long curve of his body. Reaching over her hip, he lifted one of the small, toppled cups. The china, when he lifted it, seemed incongruous in the bigness of his hand. Carefully he placed the saucer upon the shelf and nestled the cup into it.

"Such fragile things," he said with a sigh.

"Like love," she said and kept very close to the security of his chest.

"And babies."

She turned in his arms. "Babies aren't fragile, Everett. They're the toughest things in the world. They can take anything. It's the parents who break so easily."

Unable to even explain how terribly she loved him, or how heavy her despair had been at seeing him hurt, she traced the set of his jaw. "I will give you a daughter, my love. She'll be the pride of your life."

Grinning down at the beauty he found irresistible, he shook his head. "Nothing can come before you, Jenny, not a dozen daughters. You are my roots, sweetheart. Today, when I felt them being pulled up, I knew just how deep they go. How can I thank you for what you've given me this day?"

Jenny looked at herself as a thief, not as a giver of gifts. "I kept searching for ways to tell you, and then today, when I realized I was . . ."

"Today," he muttered, hearing the single faint chime of the tall clock in the hall, "today is our wedding day, the beginning of the rest of our lives. And I will be a father."

As he said the last words, he got to his feet. He swept her up in his arms.

"I will be a father," he said contentedly, eyes burning as he gazed down at her. He began walking with her to the master bedroom, her robe and his clothes forgotten.

"I will be a father," he said again, simply because he liked the sound of it.

And then again, as he laid her carefully upon their bed and fit his warmth to her warmth: "I will be a father."

There were no secrets between them any longer.

"For richer or for poorer, in sickness and in health, until death us do part."

Jenny hardly heard any of her wedding ceremony. She was brimming with the smell of flowers, the rich reverberations of the rector's tone, the knowledge that Jeffrey stood approvingly behind her, the sight of Dave's jaw, the firm grip of Everett's hand.

When the rector said, "You may kiss the bride," she started, eyes wide.

Everett dipped his head beneath the brim of her hat. "It's you and me and the willow tree," he whispered, and gently took her lips.

She felt the roots of that old tree now, reaching from the past to this place. And their own roots were sinking down together to grow strong—from day to day, season to season. The congratulations that seemed to come from everywhere once they reached the door of the church made her head reel. Her children clung to her, and over their heads Jenny met the brimming eyes of her mother. Mildred's happiness was like a pillar, strong and permanent.

"The wedding was neat, Mom," Stephen chirped, taking her bouquet and tossing it into the air and catching it again.

"Wasn't it though?" she said and lovingly kissed his forehead.

Jeffrey wriggled himself between Everett and her. Screwing up his beautiful face, he shrugged craftily at Everett. "I know it's your wedding day and all"—he choked back a prankish giggle—"but you wouldn't like to go to the arcade and play Pac-Man, would you?"

Two pairs of adult eyes—one richly brown, the other a brilliant blue—narrowed at him. Everett slipped an arm about his much-adored bride. He pretended a growl. "Out of the way, kid. You bother me."

"Just askin'," Jeffrey laughed. "Just askin'."

MORE ROMANCE FOR
A SPECIAL WAY TO RELAX
$1.95 each

2 ☐ Hastings	21 ☐ Hastings	41 ☐ Halston	60 ☐ Thorne
3 ☐ Dixon	22 ☐ Howard	42 ☐ Drummond	61 ☐ Beckman
4 ☐ Vitek	23 ☐ Charles	43 ☐ Shaw	62 ☐ Bright
5 ☐ Converse	24 ☐ Dixon	44 ☐ Eden	63 ☐ Wallace
6 ☐ Douglass	25 ☐ Hardy	45 ☐ Charles	64 ☐ Converse
7 ☐ Stanford	26 ☐ Scott	46 ☐ Howard	65 ☐ Cates
8 ☐ Halston	27 ☐ Wisdom	47 ☐ Stephens	66 ☐ Mikels
9 ☐ Baxter	28 ☐ Ripy	48 ☐ Ferrell	67 ☐ Shaw
10 ☐ Thiels	29 ☐ Bergen	49 ☐ Hastings	68 ☐ Sinclair
11 ☐ Thornton	30 ☐ Stephens	50 ☐ Browning	69 ☐ Dalton
12 ☐ Sinclair	31 ☐ Baxter	51 ☐ Trent	70 ☐ Clare
13 ☐ Beckman	32 ☐ Douglass	52 ☐ Sinclair	71 ☐ Skillern
14 ☐ Keene	33 ☐ Palmer	53 ☐ Thomas	72 ☐ Belmont
15 ☐ James	35 ☐ James	54 ☐ Hohl	73 ☐ Taylor
16 ☐ Carr	36 ☐ Dailey	55 ☐ Stanford	74 ☐ Wisdom
17 ☐ John	37 ☐ Stanford	56 ☐ Wallace	75 ☐ John
18 ☐ Hamilton	38 ☐ John	57 ☐ Thornton	76 ☐ Ripy
19 ☐ Shaw	39 ☐ Milan	58 ☐ Douglass	77 ☐ Bergen
20 ☐ Musgrave	40 ☐ Converse	59 ☐ Roberts	78 ☐ Gladstone

MORE ROMANCE FOR
A SPECIAL WAY TO RELAX

$2.25 each

79 ☐ Hastings	85 ☐ Beckman	91 ☐ Stanford	97 ☐ Shaw
80 ☐ Douglass	86 ☐ Halston	92 ☐ Hamilton	98 ☐ Hurley
81 ☐ Thornton	87 ☐ Dixon	93 ☐ Lacey	99 ☐ Dixon
82 ☐ McKenna	88 ☐ Saxon	94 ☐ Barrie	100 ☐ Roberts
83 ☐ Major	89 ☐ Meriwether	95 ☐ Doyle	101 ☐ Bergen
84 ☐ Stephens	90 ☐ Justin	96 ☐ Baxter	102 ☐ Wallace

LOOK FOR *THUNDER AT DAWN* BY PATTI BECKMAN
AVAILABLE IN AUGUST AND
SUMMER COURSE IN LOVE BY CAROLE HALSTON
IN SEPTEMBER.

SILHOUETTE SPECIAL EDITION, Department SE/2
1230 Avenue of the Americas
New York, NY 10020

Please send me the books I have checked above. I am enclosing $_____
(please add 50¢ to cover postage and handling. NYS and NYC residents
please add appropriate sales tax). Send check or money order—no cash or
C.O.D.'s please. Allow six weeks for delivery.

NAME _____

ADDRESS _____

CITY _____ STATE/ZIP _____

Silhouette Special Edition

Coming Next Month

Wild Is The Heart by Abra Taylor

Tory Allworth knew the sea was Luc Devereux's lifeblood, but the same inevitability that made the waves crash against the cliffs made Tory challenge the sea for his love.

My Loving Enemy by Pat Wallace

Once Linda had been afraid to lose herself in Judd's arms. Now, however, when it seemed the tall Texan no longer wanted her, she realized Judd's arms were the only place she wanted to be.

Fair Exchange by Tracy Sinclair

Australia had never figured in Leslie's plans until she inherited an outback ranch and came into conflict with Raider MacKenzie. At first he wanted her land . . . but then he wanted her all-too-vulnerable heart.

Never Too Late by Nancy John

Grant Kilmartin had been so busy building his construction company that he had given little thought to building relationships, until he met Natalie. They clashed professionally, but personally they were in perfect harmony.

Flower Of The Orient by Erin Ross

Lisa loved everything about Japan with one exception: Keith Brannon, the man who was pitted against her beloved uncle in business. So why was he the only man she saw in her dreams?

No Other Love by Jeanne Stephens

Their lives had taken different paths—Tyler had gone to a small West Virginia town; Kristal to Houston. But miles were nothing when Kristal learned that Tyler was hurt—and when they came together for the second time, they knew it would be forever.